Gifted Children Speak Out

Gifted Children Speak Out

James R. Delisle

Walker and Company
New York

Copyright © 1984 by James R. Delisle

All rights reserved. No part of this book may be reproduced or transmitted in any form or by any means, electric or mechanical, including photocopying, recording, or by any information storage and retrieval system, without permission in writing from the publisher.

First published in the United States of America
in 1984 by the Walker Publishing Company, Inc.

This edition printed in 1986.

Published simultaneously in Canada by John Wiley & Sons
Canada, Limited, Rexdale, Ontario.

Library of Congress Cataloging in Publication Data
Main entry under title:

Gifted children speak out.

    Bibliography: p.
      1. Gifted children—Education—United States.
2. Gifted children—United States—Attitudes.   I. Delisle, James R.
LC3993.9.G553   1984   371.95   83-42916
ISBN 0-8027-0752-1

Library of Congress Catalog Card Number: 83-42916

Printed in the United States of America

10 9 8 7 6 5 4 3 2

To Debby and Matthew,
for their continuous love and sharing.

ACKNOWLEDGMENTS

Gifted Children Speak Out has been made the complete volume that it is thanks to the assistance and advice of many friends and colleagues, including:

Jim Alvino, Editor-in-Chief of *Gifted Children Newsletter*, for publishing a summary of this book's contents in his publication.

Ruthan Brodsky, Editor of *The Roeper Review,* and the staff, faculty, and students of the Roeper City and Country School in Bloomfield Hills, Michigan, for their help in obtaining responses to several questionnaires.

Carolyn Callahan, 1982–83 President of *The Association for the Gifted* (TAG) and the TAG Executive Board members, for their permission to reprint one of my questionnaires in the TAG newsletter, *Update*.

Marjorie Craig and Gail Robinson, of the *American Association for Gifted Children,* for their help in establishing the preliminary outline and format of this book.

Roxanne Cramer, National Coordinator, Gifted Children Programs of *American Mensa,* for her help in printing one of my pupil questionnaires in her organization's newsletter.

Marvin Gold, Publisher of *G/C/T Magazine* and *Chart Your Course Magazine,* for his assistance in publicizing my initial efforts at obtaining children's responses.

Gina Ginsberg-Riggs, Executive Director of the *Gifted Child Society, Inc.,* for her help in obtaining student responses.

The Kent (Ohio) City School System, for sponsoring several workshops that helped establish my book's data base.

Special thanks to Elizabeth Valentine and the students of James B. Conant School, Bloomfield Hills, Michigan, for their tremendous support and contributions in completing this book. To Sandy Tsai, Susan del Gaudio, Sarah Blake, Michelle Frank, Julie Funk, Peter Morse, Marc Velilla, and Alex Woolf I owe a special debt of gratitude.

In addition, I thank the hundreds of individuals—parents, teachers, editors—who took the time and made the effort to contribute children's work for consideration in *Gifted Children Speak Out.*

CONTENTS

FOREWORD

INTRODUCTION

PART I: Speaking Out

PART II: Discussion Guide and Classroom Activities

FOREWORD

Many authors dedicate their works by acknowledging those "without whose help this book might not have been written." In my case, *Gifted Children Speak Out* would not have been produced at all were it not for the talented young writers whose comments fill these pages. During the past eleven months I have received responses to questionnaires from over 6,000 youngsters about the high points and hassles of being gifted. Children ages 5 to 13 were invited to respond—and respond they did!

More than 4,000 children completed survey forms I had placed in The Association for the Gifted's *Update* publication, the MENSA *Bulletin, Chart Your Course* (a magazine devoted entirely to the words and artwork of children) and any of the dozen newsletters for parents and teachers of the gifted that printed one of my eight questionnaires. The children who responded to these questionnaires lived as nearby as New York and as far removed from my former Connecticut home as Alaska, Georgia, New Mexico, British Columbia, and Puerto Rico. An additional 2,000 responses were solicited by me directly at local, state, and national conferences on gifted child education at which I distributed survey forms between October, 1982 and April, 1983. In all, 37 states and territories are represented in my survey, as well as Canada, Germany, and Australia.

Gifted Children Speak Out is a composite of the perceptions and attitudes that thousands of young people expressed on the subject of intellectual or artistic talent. In compiling this book, I have tried to select responses that most clearly and succinctly expressed particular ideas. At the same time, I have tried to present a range of responses representative of the entire spectrum of thoughts presented to me. The little editing I have done relates to spelling, not content. In this regard, you may read a response that seems illogical or imprecise. For example, the 13-year-old girl from Georgia, in Chapter 1, says that she found out she was gifted at birth when "the doctor told my mother and my mother told me." Although this answer may sound farfetched—a well-maintained piece of family folklore—it is valid nonetheless, as it is a child's perception of her own abilities which, in her mind, is accurate and real.

As of mid-1983, responses from children continue to arrive in my mailbox at the rate of about ten per week. Now, there will usually be a note attached by a parent or teacher which reads "Sorry this is so late, but I just got a chance to read my months-old newsletter—hope these responses will help." Indeed, they do help, for although they are now too late for inclusion in this book, each response still gets my full attention, and its young author my deepest thanks. Without the help of 6,000 of his or her contemporaries, *Gifted Children Speak Out* would have remained unwritten.

James R. Delisle
Kent, Ohio; August, 1983

INTRODUCTION

Gifted Children Speak Out is divided into two main sections. "Part I: Speaking Out" is a compilation of gifted children's answers to questions about their abilities and their views of these abilities. Part I has eight chapters, each reviewing one area of concern to gifted children—friends, school, parents, and the like. The exact question I asked on my surveys introduces the children's responses. These are arranged according to the ages of the children. This section of the book is meant to be read by children and their teachers and parents.

"Part II: Discussion Guide and Classroom Activities" is a series of activities and discussion questions designed for use by adults to review with children the contents of Part I. A simple cross-referencing system has been designed so that each section of children's responses in Part I corresponds to a section of activities in Part II.

In addition, there are several general activities in Part II listed as "Topics for Further Discussion." These ideas may be used to supplement any activity in a given chapter.

For the most part, the suggestions listed in Part II are appropriate for *groups* of children. The activities are intended for use with children identified as gifted and who are in educational programs designed to meet their special learning needs. Parents whose children are involved in after-school or weekend programs for the gifted, or who themselves are involved in parent education workshops may also find the activities useful. It is obvious that the teacher or parent using the activities knows his or her group of children better than I; thus, it is up to the reader's discretion to pick those activities that are most appropriate for a particular group.

A final comment: I have found that the best way to discuss giftedness with children is to first have them read the comments in a particular section of Part I. Then, ask the youngsters to express their general reactions to what they just read. Follow this discussion with one of the activities suggested in Part II, or devise some of your own, if that seems more appropriate.

PART I

Speaking Out

CHAPTER 1

Defining Giftedness

THOUGHTS

I think about
happy thoughts
And thoughts that make me cry,
I think about
angry thoughts
And though I don't know why
I think about mixed up thoughts
Of sad, of glad, of fear,
And sometimes I think about
The fact that I can think

GIRL, 8, FLORIDA

Our discussion of giftedness begins with a definition of the term. Once defined, giftedness is examined in relation to self. Thus, the first set of questions focuses on the basics: "What is giftedness?"; "Am I gifted?"; "How do I know I 'have it'?"

Following these preliminaries, the children respond to questions that address personal reactions to being gifted. Here, many children focus on the word itself—gifted—and the positive and negative impressions of this label and its implications.

Next, the youngsters comment on ways in which they regard themselves as similar to and different from their agemates. Some children highlight attitudes, while others examine behaviors that earmark them as both "special" and "a regular kid."

Finally, the need for gifted programs in schools is addressed. Many of the children respond positively to the idea of special education for bright

3

students, while others see potential inequities and flaws. Finally, children express opinions about gifted programs in which they are currently enrolled.

Question A: What Do You Think Being Gifted Means?

Gifted means being selected to attend a resource room because of your behavior and your ability to think and learn easier than others.

BOY, 9, ARKANSAS

. . . being able to think clearly.   GIRL, 9, GEORGIA

Being gifted means being able to comprehend and do things the average person does not know how to or does not want to know how to do. Being gifted also means having to do harder, more advanced work. To be frank and simple, being gifted is when you're more intelligent than most.

GIRL, 10, MICHIGAN

I know what the word gifted means, but from my point of view, I think most of the time it's used wrong. People tend to use the word gifted to describe a person good in school. Gifted *really* describes a person who is exceptionally good in anything, whether it's running or piano playing or reading. Everyone is gifted in some way.   GIRL, 10, INDIANA

It means you can do lots of things without help from grownups.

GIRL, 10, ARIZONA

I think smart and gifted are *totally* different. Being smart is just being able to answer questions and answer dates. Being gifted means you have an imagination and spirit and you are able to think creatively.

GIRL, 10, OHIO

I think being gifted must mean being especially good in the arts as well as in the academic field. Some kids think that it just means being in an academically-talented program, but a girl in my class with an IQ of 128 who is very good in art is automatically "not gifted" because you need an IQ of 130 to be in our gifted program. That's dumb.

                                                    BOY, 10, CONNECTICUT

Gifted people are smart. They usually know good from bad. They also have a lot of self-confidence. What this is leading up to is gifted people will usually do what they feel is right, even under peer pressure.

                                                    GIRL, 12, CONNECTICUT

. . . it means you are creative, original and have good leadership qualities.
                                                    GIRL, 12, GEORGIA

I think being gifted means having a special gift from God. I feel that if you are gifted, you are on Earth to fulfill a need that (maybe) other people can't fulfill.
                                                    GIRL, 12, ARKANSAS

I think it means being smart, having a wonderful imagination and being different.
                                                    GIRL, 12, ARKANSAS

A gifted child is one who will explore new things, a child who will seek to find answers and won't give up too easily.
                                                    GIRL, 12, GEORGIA

. . . a brain that works overtime.
                                                    GIRL, 12, GEORGIA

. . . that extra bit ahead of everybody else.
                                                    BOY, 12, MICHIGAN

. . . you have the ability to achieve greater goals than others.
                                                    BOY, 12, GEORGIA

Being gifted means having a talent in a special sport, field or just having a brain equal to Einstein or higher. But when I picture someone being gifted, I think of someone like John McEnroe or Beethoven, *not* someone in seventh grade.
                                                    GIRL, 12, ARKANSAS

Gifted is something that is hard to put down in print on paper. It is *definitely not*, in my mind, someone who is just a straight "A" student, though that might be one of the criteria. You must have that extra bit more of motivation that most kids don't have. You must be able to grasp complicated concepts and ideas easily and you must be responsible. Giftedness may not be something you always cherish, for it's a burden in many ways. But, being gifted, I find I have that urge to learn.

BOY, 12, MICHIGAN

Question B: Are You Gifted?

"YES"

I think I am gifted. I can read and understand arithmetic, science and social studies better than most people (but I'm terrible in gym).

GIRL, 9, BRITISH COLUMBIA

I think I'm smarter than other kids my age because when my teacher is giving a spelling test and it's time for me to go to my gifted program, she speeds up for me and the other kids can't keep up.

GIRL, 9, ALASKA

Yes, I am gifted, because my mind can store mathematical facts.

BOY, 9, GEORGIA

I think I am far more intelligent than the average student. I can think, work, draw, do poetry, write stories, read, learn, express myself and speak in front of people better than the average student.

GIRL, 10, BRITISH COLUMBIA

Yes, I am gifted, and I'm not bragging, either. I think I can do my work better and that I have a high creativity level.

GIRL, 10, GEORGIA

I do think I am smarter than most kids my age, but in only one way: I put my brain to use and make it do what everyone's brain *can* do if they would try to do it, or care.   GIRL, 11, NEW YORK

I think I am smart because I get good grades, I do good work, I am in a gifted program, I read a lot, I study and I think things through. I find my work easier than others do. Almost everything I do I seem to do well.

GIRL, 11, ARKANSAS

. . . I do notice that I am more comfortable working at high levels than most of my classmates.   BOY, 11, WEST GERMANY

. . . in a sensitive way, yes, I am gifted.   BOY, 12, GEORGIA

I think I am smart. At least that's what everyone tells me. I can read better than most kids my age and I write stories pretty well.

BOY, 12, ONTARIO

I've never really considered myself a genius but yes, I think I'm smart because I always seem to know the answer to the question no matter what the question might be.   BOY, 13, GEORGIA

"No"

No, I don't think I'm smarter than kids in my regular class. I have just been exposed to more, having had four older brothers and sisters.

BOY, 10, NEW YORK

I don't think I'm gifted because I can always learn something from others.   GIRL, 10, CONNECTICUT

I'm not gifted, just a little above average. People who are gifted are the ones that enter high school when they are thirteen.

GIRL, 12, GEORGIA

I really don't think I am any more gifted than any of my friends; I just work very hard at everything I do and usually I do very well.

GIRL, 12, ILLINOIS

No, I'm not gifted . . . I just think that my brain has been trained better
than most.   BOY, 12, CONNECTICUT

"IT DEPENDS"

. . . it depends on what you mean by gifted. I'm not what you would call
brilliant, but I'm not dumb either. I do get some nice comments on my
reading abilities, though.   GIRL, 8, ILLINOIS

I am smart in some things, like football and dominoes, and unsmart in
other subjects, like writing.   BOY, 8, GEORGIA

To be considered "smart" wouldn't be much of a task for most boys and
girls if they would only try.   BOY, 10, OHIO

I really don't *feel* smarter than all the other kids in my school, but I realize that I must be because I am in a program for talented children at school.
                                                       GIRL, 11, KENTUCKY

I know that I'm smarter than some kids in some fields—such as theatre
(when *they* say every word the same way) and creative writing (when every
other word of theirs is something like "nice" or "big"), but I also know
that in science there are many far ahead of me, and when it comes to physical education, I'm lost!   GIRL, 11, NEW YORK

In my class I'm at the top, but I know that there are people who are in
other schools who may be a lot smarter than me.
                                                       BOY, 11, WEST GERMANY

I believe I was born with a special gift but I don't believe I have quite
found it yet.   BOY, 13, GEORGIA

I do not feel that I am smarter than anybody else. I feel that a person has
to care about his intellectual being enough to study and pay attention. The

people who are ''smart'' are the ones who are able to grasp the importance
of this.   BOY, 13, KENTUCKY

Question C: How Did You Find Out That You Were Gifted?

I found out in nursery school when I was the only one who could read.
                                                GIRL, 7, ARKANSAS

When I passed the gifted test my mommy told me.
                                                GIRL, 7, LOUISIANA

. . . in a letter.   BOY, 8, ARKANSAS

When I was in nursery school I read to the class. That's how I knew.
                                                GIRL, 8, TEXAS

I learned I was gifted when second grade was easy.
                                                BOY, 9, TEXAS

I found out I was gifted in nursery school when I was told I was skipping
kindergarten.   BOY, 10, CONNECTICUT

. . . in first grade in a first/second mixed class. I would use big words
and even the second graders didn't know what I meant.
                                                GIRL, 10, MARYLAND

I learned I was gifted from my mother. (Intelligence is hereditary in our
family.)   GIRL, 10, LOUISIANA

I learned I was gifted on September 12, 1982. I found out when I got a
letter from my teacher.   BOY, 10, BRITISH COLUMBIA

. . . in grade four, although I had the suspicion since grade two.
                                              BOY, 10, BRITISH COLUMBIA

My family learned that I was gifted when I was two years old and my mother's friend gave me a grade 8 puzzle and I finished it in twenty minutes.   BOY, 11, CONNECTICUT

In third grade. I was in school on a Tuesday afternoon and my teacher called me into the hall and broke it to me easy.

BOY, 11, GEORGIA

I think I first knew I was gifted when I was in kindergarten and could read when most people couldn't. But the first time I heard "gifted" used was probably when I was going into third grade. There was a type of summer school for gifted children that I went to.

GIRL, 11, INDIANA

I first figured it out in first grade when I was starting to pass everyone in the class.   BOY, 11, NORTH CAROLINA

When I was in first grade I had a series of tests that other children didn't take. My scores were sent home one day and my mother showed me my IQ and told me my scores and that I would be in a special class because I was smart.   BOY, 11, GEORGIA

. . . I would read my brother's school papers when he brought them home.   GIRL, 11, NEBRASKA

. . . in second grade I took a gifted persons test.

GIRL, 12, GEORGIA

I learned I was gifted in fourth grade when our program for gifted children started. All kids who showed extra intelligence were recommended for it by teachers and parents.   GIRL, 12, ARKANSAS

. . . when I was two. My mom told me that I read Donald Duck books to my brother, who was one.   GIRL, 12, MISSISSIPPI

. . . in second grade; it was announced over the intercom.

GIRL, 12, GEORGIA

My parents recognized me very early, but I wasn't tested until fourth grade.   BOY, 12, ARKANSAS

. . . ever since I've been going to school, people have been telling me I'm talented.   GIRL, 12, ARKANSAS

I found out in third grade. I always finished my work and would disturb others because I had nothing to do.   GIRL, 12, NORTH CAROLINA

I've been in a gifted program since fourth grade but I didn't know I was "gifted" until sixth grade when we were given these pamphlets on what being gifted really meant.   GIRL, 13, GEORGIA

I discovered being gifted on my own, more or less, because I taught myself how to read when I was in kindergarten, and from then on I always seemed to do better than everyone (except in athletics).
                                    BOY, 13, GEORGIA

. . . when I was first born. My doctor told my mother and my mother told me.   GIRL, 13, GEORGIA

Question D: How Are You the Same as and Different from Other Children Your Age?

I enjoy playing the same games as my classmates, but I also enjoy doing harder work than my friends. Also, I'm different because I love homework.
                                    GIRL, 7, LOUISIANA,

All children have minds but we look different and think differently.
                                    GIRL, 7, ARKANSAS

. . . I'm different because I can understand jokes and riddles.
                                    GIRL, 7, GEORGIA

I think all the children in my class can do most anything I can do but I can probably understand questions more quickly than most of them.

GIRL, 9, NORTH CAROLINA

I am the same as other children in my classroom because we are all funny and smart. I'm different because some others are kinder than me.

BOY, 9, CONNECTICUT

I'm just different because I'm a little smarter, but that's not to say I'm really any *better* than anyone else.   BOY, 9, GEORGIA

I'm the same because I get into trouble for talking and I like to go to lunch and visit. I'm different because I don't like recess—I'd rather be working on a project.   BOY, 9, ARKANSAS

I can assimilate information well. I usually only need things explained once. But I make mistakes like everyone else and I ask questions when I don't understand.   GIRL, 10, GEORGIA

I love to read and I could read all day long. Kids think I am weird because I read so much. But if that makes me different, I plan on staying that way.   GIRL, 10, KENTUCKY

I am the same as other kids in that we know a lot of things and we can think logically, but the difference lies in how we interpret things and how creative we are. Another difference is how we show our knowledge of things, beyond just knowing the answer.   BOY, 10, OHIO

. . . I enjoy quiet rather than screaming, but sometimes I still jump on my bike and burn off in the hills to get dirty. That's another thing the same about kids—dirt.   GIRL, 10, BRITISH COLUMBIA

Outside of my gifted program I'm just a regular kid with the same problems and questions as other kids. I'm not really different, it's just that I'm in a higher level than the average for a sixth grader.

GIRL, 10, GEORGIA

I used to think (and sometimes still do think) that my ideas are weird. My friends don't have ideas, well, as deep as mine.

GIRL, 11, LOUISIANA

I think about the same as others in my class except I *want* to learn and they just want to rush through everything so they can have fun. I'm different from them in many ways. I can pick up a book and really get interested. They just pick it up and put it down. I also think I am *determined* to do certain things—they just do it if they can.   GIRL, 11, NORTH CAROLINA

I like to talk and laugh just like other kids. I'm different because sometimes I think the "in crowd" is a little bit silly.

GIRL, 11, ARKANSAS

I still make mistakes and sometimes get bad grades. I know a little more about the world because I lived in Europe, and I am a little ahead of them in science because I'm from a different school system.

GIRL, 11, GEORGIA

I really don't feel I'm different from anyone else. I might be a little chubby but I don't feel like I'm any different.

GIRL, 11, ARKANSAS

I think I am as athletic as anyone, but I'm different because I think a problem through and others write the first thing they think is right.

BOY, 11, ARKANSAS

We are all pretty smart but we are different (very different) in personalities.   BOY, 12, GEORGIA

The difference is that I enjoy doing schoolwork and the others don't.

GIRL, 12, GEORGIA

I'm different because I can relate to gifted people better.

GIRL, 12, GEORGIA

All of my friends have some of the same strong points I have, while many of them excel in areas I do not. As long as I help them when they have problems and I let them help me when I'm stuck, it works out fine.

GIRL, 12, ILLINOIS

I ask the same questions, but on a more intellectual basis. I have a larger vocabulary, though, and a different sense of humor.

BOY, 13, GEORGIA

I'm the same because I'm just a regular kid and I'm different because in most cases, when a teacher calls on me I can answer right away, where most kids have to think a second.   GIRL, 13, GEORGIA

I don't really do much different, but I challenge my teachers more and argue points and insights more than the other kids (who take the teachers' word for everything). I love to argue with teachers, but not just for the sake of arguing.   GIRL, 13, OHIO

I feel that I relate to adults relatively better than others my own age. I also feel that I have more ambition than most people my age. On the outside, though, I'm pretty much the same—I enjoy going places with friends and having a good time. But if I don't have my homework done, I can't enjoy myself, while most people my age don't let that bother them.

GIRL, 13, GEORGIA

Question E: What Is Your Opinion About Being Gifted? What Is Your Reaction to the Term "Gifted"?

REACTIONS TO BEING GIFTED

I've always felt good about being bright.   BOY, 7, CONNECTICUT

. . . I feel very happy and sometimes I cry for happiness.

GIRL, 8, OHIO

My abilities are something special but I hate when someone makes a big deal out of them.   GIRL, 10, NEW YORK

Being gifted bothers me. I just like being one of the gang, just another student.   BOY, 11, GEORGIA

I am constantly being reminded how smart I am and it's getting pretty sickening.   GIRL, 11, ILLINOIS

I would like to make a point of saying what I have often said: "Please, God, don't let me be normal!", although it can be lonely when you're the only kid who wants to be different. Believe me, I *am* different, but I'm more in control of it than most other kids.   GIRL, 11, NEW YORK

Being called gifted is fine, but when a teacher brings it up I feel like an outsider, considering most of my friends aren't gifted. One child in class who has an I.Q. of about one million (exaggeration) often talks to "not gifted" kids like "I'm gifted and you're not, so ha! ha!" So, in other words, it's OK for teacher-talk and recommendations for things, but around my class "gifted" is almost a kind of mean, discriminating word.

BOY, 11, CONNECTICUT

THE TERM "GIFTED": "I LIKE IT"

I don't mind being called gifted as long as I'm not stereotyped as being perfect.   BOY, 9, GEORGIA

Giftedness is being in kindergarten and having to miss free play in art to go to first grade reading.   GIRL, 12, WEST GERMANY

I really do not mind being called gifted. It is not an absurd name like some people think, and it doesn't embarrass me. It is sort of like a praise when you're called gifted.   GIRL, 11, GEORGIA

I like being called gifted but only if it doesn't interfere with my friends.

For example, I'm sure most people would be annoyed if their friend was constantly called "gifted" while no one said a thing to them.

GIRL, 11, INDIANA

I like being called gifted because it makes me feel special, but when I think about it I don't want to be gifted because I want to be the same as my friends.   BOY, 11, CONNECTICUT

I'd rather be called gifted than smarty pants!

BOY, 12, GEORGIA

I think the word gifted is perfect, because it means we have a "gift" to understand things others don't.   GIRL, 13, GEORGIA

THE TERM "GIFTED": "I DON'T LIKE IT"

I do not like being called gifted; it's embarassing and it's like bragging.

BOY, 9, NEW MEXICO

No, I don't like being called gifted because it makes other people think you're a genius. I would rather be called a better thinker.

BOY, 10, BRITISH COLUMBIA

I don't like being called gifted. When I think of a gifted person, I think of an eerie old man with a long beard, little spectacles and lots of wrinkles. A name I would like better would be "over average student." I like this name better because it doesn't make me sound like a genius.

BOY, 10, OHIO

Being called gifted isn't something you like or dislike, it's really something you cope with whether you like it or not. I would rather be called "talented" or "well above average" because it would sound better to say "She is well above average in her schoolwork" than to say "She is gifted in her schoolwork."   GIRL, 10, NORTH CAROLINA

I don't like being called gifted because people expect too much of me.

GIRL, 10, LOUISIANA

"Gifted" sounds too powerful. I think the term "capable children" is better because it doesn't sound as if you have E.S.P.

GIRL, 11, BRITISH COLUMBIA

I do not like being called gifted because along with that I get called "brain." I like the word "special" better than "gifted" because it does not necessarily refer to being very smart.   GIRL, 11, LOUISIANA

I think one of the main reasons I don't like the word gifted is because of the way teachers use it. When a teacher is talking to another teacher, she'll say "THAT child is gifted!" in a tone that sounds as though she should worship the word and be honored that she has a gifted student in her class.

GIRL, 11, CONNECTICUT

. . . forget "gifted," and use "intelligent"; it's more subtle.

BOY, 11, ARKANSAS

I don't like being called gifted because it makes me feel like an object and not my own individual person. I don't think we should be "called" anything. We were just born smarter than others and can't help it. When people call me a "gifted child" it makes me angry.

GIRL, 12, GEORGIA

I do not like being called gifted. It makes me think something is wrong with me. I don't know of any other word to replace "gifted" but I wish someone would think of something.   GIRL, 12, GEORGIA

I really feel uncomfortable with the word gifted. It makes me feel like I am covered with wrapping paper and tied up in a bow.

GIRL, 12, CONNECTICUT

Sometimes people think "gifted" means stuck up and they think that you are going to make fun of their grades because they don't make as good grades as you do.   GIRL, 13, MISSISSIPPI

Question F: Some Schools Have Special Programs and Teachers for Gifted Students. Is This a Good Idea?

"YES"

Gifted programs help smart people get smarter.

GIRL, 8, NEW YORK

Yes, gifted programs are a good idea because kids that are smart at something should not do things that are too easy for them.

BOY, 8, NEW YORK

I think gifted classes are a good idea because kids get bored in school and might start getting bad grades.   BOY, 9, NEW YORK

I think that all schools should have gifted programs because they give gifted children a chance to *really* use their brain.

BOY, 9, OHIO

Yes, because it helps gifted students to learn more and to "keep up" with their brains.   GIRL, 11, PUERTO RICO

I think gifted programs are a good idea because gifted children should be worked to their full potential. Besides, it gives the kids something "extra" to do.   GIRL, 11, CONNECTICUT

. . . gifted programs give kids a chance to stay smart.

BOY, 11, GEORGIA

. . . if you're in a class that's easy, you're not learning anything.

BOY, 11, NEW YORK

Kids in a gifted program will get to do lots of things that are fun and they'll get to learn new things that could help them to become a success (like writing a book and having it published).

GIRL, 11, NEW YORK

. . . I like to be around children who are as intelligent as I am.

BOY, 11, NORTH CAROLINA

. . . the people who *can* do harder work or *can* go to special classes should be able to *get* what they deserve.   GIRL, 12, NEW YORK

Some teachers don't teach enough so enrichment classes are good for getting more information. These enrichment classes can be more fun and exciting.   GIRL, 12, NEW YORK

. . . some people don't like their classmates or teachers and need to get away for part of the day. They already know most of the work in their classrooms so they need a special program.   BOY, 12, NEW YORK

I believe you should have a special class for special kids so that they can learn faster. Because when a child is kept from learning, he or she will become frustrated.   GIRL, 12, MICHIGAN

Schools should have gifted programs, but also they should have other special programs (such as art, physical education, music, etc.) for the rest of the kids who have other special talents.   GIRL, 12, ILLINOIS

I think it is a good idea to have special programs for smart kids. They prepare kids for what the future may bring and they reward those who have the gift of intelligence.   GIRL, 12, CALIFORNIA

I believe that special programs are important because without them I wouldn't be able to learn anything extra and I wouldn't have any competition.   BOY, 12, CALIFORNIA

. . . without the gifted program, I would have no reason to go to school.

GIRL, 12, NEW YORK

Gifted programs break up the monotony of the day. Also, kids can pursue things that if the program did not exist they would not be able to do.

GIRL, 12, NEW YORK

I think a gifted program stimulates a gifted student's mind to learn about other gifted children and how they feel about being gifted.

GIRL, 12, ALABAMA

Some kids need some time to "break away" and explore the inner reaches of their minds to find out about other worlds, cultures and new ideas.   GIRL, 13, NEW YORK

. . . it isn't fair to the children who are already smart to have to listen in the regular class to things they already know.

GIRL, 13, NEW YORK

"No"

I think that you should not have a program for children that are skilled because I think it affects the whole class and makes them feel bad. I think we could have our meetings in the classroom just as well.

GIRL, 8, ILLINOIS

No. Gifted programs make you miss your other classes and they make other kids jealous, too.   GIRL, 9, ILLINOIS

I think that maybe gifted students should have a special program but it should not take up regular classroom time. Sure, the students might be getting out of class, but we miss important lessons and we have to stay in for recess to learn them.   GIRL, 11, CONNECTICUT

Sometimes I think gifted programs are a good idea because they make kids work. But other times I don't think they are a great idea because some people that almost "made it" and have tried hard get let down. And sometimes, with all the after school activities, getting your work done that you missed when you were at the gifted program causes you to not think about what you're supposed to be thinking about.

GIRL, 11, ILLINOIS

Why not have anyone who is interested in something and has a special ability get time to work on it?

GIRL, 11, NEW YORK

Gifted programs separate the smart students from the average students even more than they are now. I was separated in kindergarten and it smelled. BOY, 12, OHIO

Gifted programs? Yes and no. Yes because it is a good idea for us to understand more and better things. No because the other kids feel like they're completely stupid because they aren't in the gifted class.

GIRL, 12, ILLINOIS

Question G: For Those of You in Gifted Programs, Write Down How You Feel about This Program.

I feel terrific working with other great minds.

GIRL, 7, ARKANSAS

I like being in a gifted program. It's nice to work with other kids who don't have to look at my papers for the right answers.

GIRL, 7, WYOMING

At first I was scared, but now I really like it.

GIRL, 8, LOUISIANA

Before gifted classes came along I was bored of the same old stuff six and a half hours a day, five days a week. I don't know where I'd be without my gifted classes. BOY, 9, CALIFORNIA

Because my gifted program lasts all day and is high level, I feel very satisfied and happy. My classmates are very interesting, we all learn from one another, and the worthwhile work we do is helping me prepare for a good career and future. BOY, 9, NEW MEXICO

. . . we have 99.7% more freedom. BOY, 10, ARIZONA

My gifted program gives me a chance to learn more, feel good about myself, and have a good time because I am accomplishing something.

                                                                BOY, 10, TEXAS

I like being in gifted because it is fun to do extra work, plus we are a small group so it is easy to concentrate.   BOY, 10, GEORGIA

. . . I can see different teachers and different kids than in my classroom. It gives me a chance to get away from work and silence. I like my gifted program a lot!   GIRL, 10, CONNECTICUT

I love my gifted program. It sort of makes me want to give an extra effort. Being in our gifted program makes me feel proud of myself.

                                                              GIRL, 11, GEORGIA

I feel very happy in my gifted program because I get bored in regular classrooms. It's fun being able to choose what you want to do. Sometimes people make fun of me for being smart, but to tell you the truth I think they're jealous.   BOY, 11, LOUISIANA

. . . it's more of a personal class. If you have a problem or if you don't really think you're getting any use out of what you're studying, you can tell your teacher and she can help you.   GIRL, 11, LOUISIANA

. . . I love it! I have to make up work, and sometimes I have to stay in for recess to get it done, but my gifted program is the brightest part of my day.   BOY, 11, NORTH CAROLINA

. . . it's real fun! I wish that everyone was intelligently smart.

                                                              GIRL, 11, ALABAMA

Being in the gifted program gives me a chance to say what I feel about something and not be laughed at. I *like* to be understood.

                                                              GIRL, 11, GEORGIA

In a regular class there is only one right answer to questions, but here there are lots of correct answers.   GIRL, 11, BRITISH COLUMBIA

. . . in a regular class a gifted person gets bored silly. We need someone
to push us beyond mediocrity.   BOY, 12, GEORGIA

. . . sometimes I like it and sometimes I don't because you are thought
of by others as "a brain."   GIRL, 12, MISSISSIPPI

I've enjoyed being in all the gifted programs I've participated in because
they are always small classes. The smaller the class, the more of a friendship you can build with others. I was able to relate better to my last year's
teacher (gifted teacher) than almost anyone I've ever known (except, of
course, my twin brother).   BOY, 12, NORTH CAROLINA

. . . I don't like it anymore. I've been in my gifted program since third
grade and now I'm in seventh; we always do the same thing and most of the
girls and a few of the boys are snobs.   BOY, 12, GEORGIA

. . . without extras like the gifted program, school turns into a monotonous circle of turn-in-your-papers, listen, ignore and be ignored.
                                               GIRL, 12, KENTUCKY

. . . it's neat; you're treated more like adults.
                                               BOY, 13, MISSISSIPPI

. . . I feel as if I'm smart enough to be anything and everything I want.
                                               GIRL, 13, GEORGIA

I enjoy the gifted class because it seems to me that we have a special
friendship for others in the class—what I mean is we get to be better friends.
Also, I enjoy having so much more independence.
                                               GIRL, 13, MISSISSIPPI

I feel that being in the gifted program I am with kids on my intellectual
level (except for a few that are geniuses and a few that act like fourth graders). I love doing activities that take a great deal of critical thinking to improve my knowledge and vocabulary. And, though I believe I have a gifted

talent, I also believe that no one knows everything, so until I am too old to think, I'll be learning.   BOY, 13, GEORGIA

. . . it gives me an hour out of every day to do the things I really enjoy and to just be "me."   GIRL, 13, GEORGIA

CHAPTER 2

Getting Along With Friends and Classmates

PROFESSOR

"Professor" 's what they call me
I'm known throughout the school
As some straight-laced goody-goody
Who never breaks a rule.
If I get in trouble
It makes the news headlines—
I guess it's a conspiracy
To be among good minds.
I wish they knew the real me,
The one that stays inside,
The one known to my "gifted" friends
But to others, stays inside.

GIRL, 13, OHIO

For this second chapter, children comment on the positive and negative reactions they get from classmates and friends about being gifted. Some report that intellectual differences make no difference ("My friends like me for what I am"), while a few state that academic talents tend to stifle relationships with anyone except other gifted children. Several children interpret negative comments from friends as being the result of jealousy, while just as many students reveal a wish that everyone could be gifted, making both school and life more fair.

25

On hiding their academic abilities from others, gifted children respond strongly both pro and con. While several see it as a technique useful in establishing peer rapport, others find it offensive to disguise their talent. Lastly, gifted children reveal some of the more hurtful reactions they get from friends who don't understand that being gifted is not something done to spite those less intelligent than they.

Question A: How Do Friends React to Your Abilities? What Do They Do or Say That Makes You Feel Good or Bad About Being Gifted?

POSITIVE REACTIONS

My friends treat me good. They say "that's a good story, Bobby" and "you're doing good in your school." They don't make me feel bad.

BOY, 6, ILLINOIS

My friends say "gee whiz, Mark, you're so darn smart—I wish I could be." My friends also make me feel good by saying "That work is better than I can do."

BOY, 7, COLORADO

. . . my good friends are happy that I have special abilities.

GIRL, 9, CALIFORNIA

My friends do not act differently to me because of my abilities. Half of my friends are gifted so they're as smart as I am. The ones that aren't gifted are nice to me—they say I'm a good worker and they say I'm smart.

BOY, 9, CALIFORNIA

My friends treat me the same as their other friends, but sometimes they compliment me and that makes me feel good.

GIRL, 10, OHIO

. . . I just fit right in. Being gifted doesn't really affect my relationship

with my friends because most of my friends are bright and they can cope
with it. BOY, 10, PENNSYLVANIA

Most of my friends act very nice to me, not because of my abilities but
because of who I am. GIRL, 10, PENNSYLVANIA

. . . they try to get me to do their work for them.
GIRL, 11, PUERTO RICO

My friends ask me for help when they don't understand something. They
don't tease or make fun of me, but appreciate my help.
BOY, 12, VIRGINIA

My friends are very kind and they are all bright. Sometimes my friends
ask me things that they don't know and then I feel very good about myself.
GIRL, 12, ILLINOIS

Most of the time my friends treat me like any other kid and that is what I
like. Sometimes they look up to me to do things—I like that too!
GIRL, 12, CALIFORNIA

My friends treat me the same as they would a not-so-gifted person. They
do not say anything to make me feel bad, but instead they compliment me
about being gifted. They tell me I am very lucky to be gifted.
GIRL, 12, CALIFORNIA

I am very lucky because I have really great friends. My friends accept me
for what I am and they don't mind when I go to a different school for my
gifted program. They don't mind when I talk to them about such topics as
science and government, instead of baseball and football.
BOY, 12, VIRGINIA

I am considerably lucky to have friends that understand it's a very precious gift to be talented and bright in many ways. Some friends of mine
compliment my work, which is nice. Others say cruel things (which I don't
care to mention). GIRL, 13, CONNECTICUT

NEGATIVE REACTIONS

One of my unfriends makes fun of me.   GIRL, 8, KANSAS

On the days I have my gifted program, Martha isn't my friend. Other days she likes me.   GIRL, 8, PENNSYLVANIA

My friend Shelly said "Whoopie-ding-bat" about being in a gifted program.   GIRL, 8, MAINE

My friends react to my abilities by calling me "school boy." They call me other names like that too. It used to bother me but now it doesn't.
                    BOY, 9, CALIFORNIA

When I play games older kids play, they say "Act your own age" and I just ignore them and walk away.   GIRL, 9, ALASKA

The kids in my class call me "bookworm" just because I read a lot more than most of the kids in my class.   BOY, 9, WYOMING

I've gotten almost all my spelling tests, reading tests, and math tests right. Some of the other kids don't at all. So, they either say "you cheated" or "the teacher spends more time with you." I really hate it. It drives me crazy.   GIRL, 9, NEW JERSEY

When we talk about report cards, my friends sometimes say I was "teacher's pet" and that's why I got straight A's. It bugs me to know my friends feel that way about me.   GIRL, 10, CALIFORNIA

. . . and what makes me feel bad is when people call me "brainy" and "Mr. Know-it-all" and quite a few other names which I dare not write!
                    BOY, 10, ILLINOIS

Last year, G.T. stood for *G*arbage and *T*rash or *G*ifted *T*urkeys. This year, when we get back from our gifted (g/t) program some kids go "YUCK! G.T.'s." It makes me feel like smacking them, but usually I don't.   GIRL, 10, LOUISIANA

. . . they treat me as if I wasn't there, they play tricks on me and they exclude me from their games.   GIRL, 10, KENTUCKY

Sometimes my friends tease me. If they don't know the answer to a question, they sometimes say, "Ask Mary, she's the brain." When I ask them to stop teasing me, they say "I would be proud if I were you." It bugs me sometimes.   GIRL, 11, VIRGINIA

Some kids say that I am smart and that I am the teacher's pet. Sometimes friends reject me, so I find other friends.   GIRL, 11, MICHIGAN

One example of peer pressure is that when I was reading the book *On Being Gifted,* I was embarrassed to leave the book on my desk during school days.   BOY, 11, MICHIGAN

If a bully or such calls me dumb, my friend will say "You're one to talk . . . Mary happens to be gifted, which is more than I can say for you!" It is sort of embarrassing.   GIRL, 11, ALABAMA

There is one girl in my class who has no respect for anyone else's feelings. She makes fun of me for being gifted. Sometimes I wish I could be dumb. Other people just expect me to do well and when I don't, they make fun of me. I wish I could be like everybody and be accepted by everyone.
                    GIRL, 11, MASSACHUSETTS

Kids I don't know tease me. Our teacher calls us "Champs" and the other kids call us "Chumps."   GIRL, 11, CALIFORNIA

Some of my friends treat me like an encyclopedia, which makes me wonder if they are friends or users.   BOY, 11, ILLINOIS

Sometimes one boy always sticks out his tongue and makes a face when I get a better grade than he does.   GIRL, 11, OHIO

Quite a few kids at the school where my gifted program is rough us up, but that's about all.   BOY, 11, CONNECTICUT

. . . they think when I go to my gifted program I go to special education, and they call me names.   BOY, 11, MAINE

Because of my abilities and being in a gifted class, some children at school don't like me. They see me as a spoiled brat but I'm really not. Maybe if they knew the real me they'd like me.

GIRL, 11, CALIFORNIA

Most of my friends are in a talented and gifted program just as I am, but some of my friends who may not be as bright as me may call me a POIN, meaning one who constantly studies and gets straight A's. That kind of gets me to feel bad because they don't understand.

BOY, 11, CONNECTICUT

Most of the kids seem to like me but sometimes I think it's because they can copy my answers. Some of them like me for myself but others treat me like some form of cast-off.   BOY, 11, OHIO

My friends sometimes feel coldly about me when I ask questions to better my knowledge. But when they have a cousin or friend from out-of-town, they show me off like I was their best friend in the world.

BOY, 12, NEW JERSEY

Eating lunch is not too pleasant when peas are flung at you and people are constantly saying "You think you're gifted? Well, I get a lot of presents for Christmas, too!" There will always be those certain jealous few you can't stand.   GIRL, 12, CONNECTICUT

I am more active in more intellectual types of groups and clubs, and for that I am sneered at, called names and looked down at. But I try not to let it get me down because I know the other kids are just jealous, but somehow this makes it difficult to participate in other activities at school (example: I am always the last one picked for a softball team in P.E.).

GIRL, 13, GEORGIA

People I know at school are jealous of my grades and how I am able to skim by in my classes and still make the honor roll at the end of every term. Despite my all-out efforts to be friendly to everyone and to "fit in" with the norm, many people brand me as a "soce" or a "teacher's pet"—both key words meaning a cross between a goody two-shoes and a little know-it-all.

GIRL, 13, WYOMING

NEUTRAL REACTIONS

One friend says that I act cool because I am in a third grade room for reading and math, but none of my other friends say anything. I don't feel I act cool.   GIRL, 7, ILLINOIS

. . . they don't even notice.   GIRL, 7, MAINE

My friends treat me like any other of their friends. I like it that way. Also, they think I'm lucky and I think so too.

GIRL, 8, OHIO

My friends don't say anything about me being different and I'm glad. When they ask me for help it makes me feel good that I can help them. I never feel bad about being gifted but sometimes I wish some other kids were more interested in some of the things I am.

GIRL, 9, CONNECTICUT

My friends really aren't jealous because a lot of them go to special classes and so they know if they tease me they'll get the same thing in return.   GIRL, 10, MAINE

Overall, they're pretty good about it, but when I get my report card they say "All *A*'s again?"   GIRL, 10, TEXAS

My friends don't really care about my being in the gifted program. If they ever say anything about it, it's something nice like "Boy, you're the smartest person I know." That makes me feel good.

BOY, 10, ILLINOIS

I don't think my friends really think anything about me because they

don't do anything to me except once in a while they don't believe me when
I say I didn't get less than a "B−" on my report card.

                                                    BOY, 11, WYOMING

My friends really don't seem to care. It doesn't seem to bother them
much unless they're just keeping it inside them.

                                                    GIRL, 11, PENNSYLVANIA

My peer group is mostly made up of gifted students. Those that aren't
don't think of us as any different. Actually, I've never stopped to think
about how I'm smarter than they are. I like to think of myself as just an average person, although grown-ups always tell me not to think that way.

                                                    GIRL, 11, ILLINOIS

Most of my friends don't have a reaction to my abilities. My best friend
is smart herself so most of the time when we're together we exchange
thoughts and knowledge.   GIRL, 11, ILLINOIS

Most of my friends have abilities, whether it be in sports, school or anything else. They don't say much about me being bright. The farthest it goes
is when they call me a brain, but everywhere you're going to get some people who are jealous.   GIRL, 12, ILLINOIS

. . . some get jealous, others call me a "brain," but my real friends
don't do either of these things—I respect them for that.

                                                    GIRL, 12, ILLINOIS

My friends don't really mind me being gifted, or at least they haven't
shown they mind. They really never say anything—good or bad.

                                                    BOY, 12, GEORGIA

A lot of times when I'm speaking, I'll get onto a subject that other kids
can't comprehend. Because of this, they will laugh and hold it against me
for several days. This really doesn't bother me, though; other than that, I
have very little problem with other kids.   BOY, 13, KENTUCKY

Question B: Are There Ever Times When You Try to "Hide" the Fact That You Are Gifted?

"YES"

Sometimes I try to hide that I'm gifted when I'm around kids not too smart, because they might think they shouldn't be around me 'cause I'm smart.   GIRL, 8, MICHIGAN

I try to hide my abilities so my friend Herman won't think I'm a show-off. And I don't like not being liked. And I am not a show-off.
                                                                 BOY, 9, ALASKA

Yes . . . from my best friend. She is not too smart and I'm afraid I'll lose my best friend if I'm smart.   GIRL, 9, KENTUCKY

. . . Sometimes we'll do an easy thing and I'll take my time to look like I'm just as puzzled as everyone else.   GIRL, 9, ILLINOIS

I try to hide I'm smart when I'm making friends with someone, because they might think I'm some kind of priss that brags about being smart.
                                                                 GIRL, 9, ALASKA

Sometimes I don't feel like I fit in so I hide that I am gifted.
                                                                 BOY, 10, KENTUCKY

Yes . . . I live in an area where there aren't any other gifted people and they tease me about being good in academic classes.
                                                                 GIRL, 10, MICHIGAN

Sometimes when my friends talk about "how hard the test was" or "I did so bad on that test" and I did well, I just don't say anything that might hurt their feelings or offend them.   GIRL, 11, MICHIGAN

Yes, many times, but especially when I'm just meeting someone. I don't want them to say "Oh, you're one of those"—so I hide it.
                                                                 GIRL, 12, CONNECTICUT

When all my classmates ask me what I got on a paper or report card and I say "never mind." They always say mean things about my doing well.

GIRL, 12, CONNECTICUT

There are times I try to act "dumb". The reason I do this is because some of my friends aren't very bright—they feel uncomfortable when I act gifted, so I act dumb to make them feel more comfortable.

BOY, 12, KENTUCKY

"No"

I think it is special to be gifted and I never hide it.

BOY, 7, MICHIGAN

I am proud to be gifted and I think others should be also. Since we were lucky enough to have a gift like this, I don't see any reason I should hide something that wonderful.   GIRL, 10, KENTUCKY

No . . . if you've got it why not use it? What is the problem with being smart?   BOY, 10, NEW YORK

I seldom try to hide the fact that I'm smart because most people don't care.   BOY, 11, NEW YORK

The only time I try to hide the fact that I am gifted is when I am with friends or other kids and want to "fit in" or be a part of a group.

BOY, 12, CONNECTICUT

I never try to hide being gifted because there is no reason to be ashamed of it.   BOY, 12, NEW YORK

No. I'm proud of the fact that I'm gifted. Since I'm not popular or pretty, I feel that I have to have something to make myself accepted, so I rely on my gifted ability.   GIRL, 12, KENTUCKY

I don't think that I should ever hide what I am. You should never hide what you are because then people will never know what you are inside. I have come to the point in my life where my friends like me for what I am. When I was in fourth grade the only reason I had friends was so they could copy off my tests.   GIRL, 13, NEW JERSEY

Question C: Is There Anything You Would Like to Share About Your Own Reactions to Being Smarter Than Some of Your Friends?

Well, sometimes someone asks me a question and I'm glad to answer it, but sometimes I'm sorry they don't know the answer themselves.
                                                        GIRL, 8, ILLINOIS

Once in a while I play young learning games just to help kids not as smart as me.   GIRL, 8, MAINE

My friend Kris keeps bugging me about going to my gifted program. He says, "I'd sure like to go to QUEST." It makes me feel good because he'd like to go. It makes me feel bad because he keeps bugging me about it.
                                                        BOY, 8, MAINE

My friend who stayed back asked me a question about a times table and I couldn't answer it. She said, "If you are gifted you should know." Then she laughed. I felt dumb.   GIRL, 8, MAINE

Math is hard for me. Once I got an "F" in math. My best friend was listening when I said "Oh, no!" She said "What are you complaining about?" I told her and also asked her what she got. She got an "A" or "B," I can't remember. I told her I thought she was a better mathematician. She said "No, I'm not. You're in the gifted program, I'm not." At that time, I wished I was very stupid.   GIRL, 10, ILLINOIS

Some of my friends act like they're as gifted as me, but they're really not. They pretend that they're doing better work and are higher in grade

levels in reading than they really are. That makes me angry that they try to
be something they're not.   BOY, 10, CONNECTICUT

If my friends ask me a question and I find I don't know the answer, they
sometimes complain and say, "I thought you were supposed to be smart."
It depends on my feelings whether I get mad or not, but usually I don't get
too upset.   GIRL, 11, CONNECTICUT

Last year when we were in P.E. and I did something real good some of
my friends would come up to me and say "Jill, you're bragging." They
came up and said that when I was just standing there! I think that was pretty
rude.   GIRL, 11, NEBRASKA

In religious class I'm the teacher's pet and I know that the other kids resent me—I know that they do by the looks they give me. Sometimes I pur-
posely don't raise my hand to answer the teacher's question.
                                                        BOY, 11, CONNECTICUT

If someone is talking about a topic and I tell them what I know about it,
they seem to think that I am bragging . . . and I don't mean for it to be that
way! I just try to share my knowledge with them but they take it that I am
bragging. Now I'm careful of who I say things in front of.
                                                        BOY, 11, CONNECTICUT

People always say to me, "I know you got 100 on that test." They expect me to say I did, and if I *didn't*, the whole class knows in five minutes.
If I *did*, they say "oh" and walk away, leaving me wondering "What kind
of crime is it to pass a test?"   GIRL, 11, CONNECTICUT

Whenever I'm doing my work and I get something right while others get
it wrong, they say "Sally's so much more smart than us." That makes me
feel good and bad at different times. It makes me feel *good* when they laugh
after they say it but it makes me feel *bad* when they make a face.
                                                        GIRL, 11, PENNSYLVANIA

One day in school another teacher needed sixth-graders to help her kids
in first grade. I didn't want to go even though I was in an eighth grade spell-

ing book. My friends teased me and said "Afraid you're going to spell a word wrong?" I got over that, but I still remember that day.

GIRL, 11, MICHIGAN

Cold shoulders, dirty looks and smirks hurt a lot more than somebody coming right out and saying something horrible.

GIRL, 11, MICHIGAN

Sometimes when I get better marks on a test than others, I ask my friend what she got. Then I tell her my mark and she says "Why should I tell you; now that you're in that gifted class all you do is brag." I don't get very mad at this—hurt, yes, but not mad. I am starting to understand why she does it, but sometimes I feel I am all alone.   GIRL, 11, BRITISH COLUMBIA

Some of my competitive friends try to do better than I do. Other friends ask that I try to speak within their vocabulary range. Some classmates think I'm square—they have a lot of stereotypes.

GIRL, 12, CONNECTICUT

I don't judge other people by their intelligence and I don't like them to judge me that way either.   GIRL, 12, GEORGIA

There will always be kids who are jealous of you so there will always be someone who will make fun of what you do. But your real friends will accept you for what you are and you shouldn't ask for more from them.

GIRL, 13, NEW JERSEY

There are times I wish people did not know I was gifted. Sometimes I want to run away from the people who harass me for being gifted. But I realize I would only be providing more problems for myself. Someday, I feel, I will learn to handle this problem.

On the other hand, when I go away to a place where people don't know me, sometimes I say or do something that makes me feel stupid. At those times, I feel like I want to yell to everyone around me, "Don't you realize I'm gifted!"   BOY, 13, KENTUCKY

CHAPTER 3

Expectations:
Yours and Others'

I think I push myself harder than my parents do. They have always accepted my getting good grades and when I get a bad grade I think I am more disappointed than my parents. When I set goals for myself they are quite high, and when I don't reach them I become downfallen, and sometimes I feel like there is no point in life and that I want to run away and who cares about school anyway. But I always get at it again and try even harder.

GIRL, 11, MICHIGAN

The questions in this chapter were designed to review the level of expectation placed upon gifted children. First, the children examine the expectations of their harshest critics: themselves. Here, gifted boys and girls discuss their own academic, social, and behavioral expectations. Next, expectations from others are reviewed, and bright children describe the wide range of reactions they hear from agemates and adults about how well gifted children should think, perform in school, or behave. As you shall read, there is a similarity between the expectations of both the children and adults.

Responses to the third question in this chapter make it clear that many gifted children consider mistakes as "OK—as long as *I'm* not the one making them." It is the rare child who accepts a mistake as a possible learning experience, or who thinks of errors as being essential to intellectual growth.

Lastly, this chapter deals with the issue of conformity. I asked the children if they had ever done anything just to go along with the crowd. Their responses vary, of course, but the consensus appears to be that the less vital the issue, the more likely the child will go along with the majority.

Question A: What Do You Expect from "A Person With Your Abilities"?

I feel the grades I get are OK unless I get an *A*– or under.

BOY, 9, RHODE ISLAND

I expect a lot of good work from myself.   GIRL, 10, ILLINOIS

Sometimes I feel like "Oh, no! What if I get a bad grade! Mom'll just kill me!" But I *know* I won't make a grade that bad, because it never has happened and it never will.   GIRL, 10, LOUISIANA

Sometimes I'm really smart, but when it matters and I goof, it breaks my heart.   GIRL, 10, NEW YORK

I am a reasonably lazy person, so I do usually just what I can get by with.

GIRL, 10, GEORGIA

I sort of like getting the highest mark because I really feel good after I've accomplished that. I feel like everything's off my back, like all that pressure.   GIRL, 10, CONNECTICUT

I love *A*'s, and the first time I got a *B,* I cried. But I only got one. No more of those *B*'s.   GIRL, 11, CONNECTICUT

I sometimes feel I need to do something all my own way, something only mine, that I can be proud of.

It might seem reasonable that it would be easy for a gifted child to get too self-conscious and expect to always get good grades. For me, it's always fear that I'll do horribly, and fearing a tirade from a teacher.

BOY, 11, MICHIGAN

I feel that I should work for a grade and then get what I deserve. I like to get A's and B's on my report card and personally won't accept anything below that.   GIRL, 11, CONNECTICUT

I've been thinking about how much an A is on any paper. How does an A show how much you study? What you do at school on a daily basis? How good is an A on any one paper? How high is an A? How I push myself to get that A. What is it?   GIRL, 11, MICHIGAN

I know if I had a test with anyone my age I would probably win hands down. People say I have too much self-confidence—but I think I have just enough.   GIRL, 11, MASSACHUSETTS

I think I am harder on myself than anyone else. For instance, if I get a B on something then I will be very disappointed. I don't think that I push myself too hard—I just get upset if I don't do well.
                                                   BOY, 11, MICHIGAN

Sometimes I wish I didn't get all A's. First, because everyone makes fun of me and second, because it shows that I'm not really being challenged. I don't do as much as I could, but I get straight A's anyway.
                                                 GIRL, 12, PENNSYLVANIA

I'm dissatisfied with myself until a project is completely understood, and then I discuss the knowledge with someone else.
                                                   BOY, 12, MICHIGAN

Over the last year it would have been a breeze to get straight A's but I held back and coasted. I don't feel too good about this.
                                                 GIRL, 12, CONNECTICUT

I'm disappointed when I fail to accomplish something but I try to accept it and try again and again until I get it right. I'm proud of high achievements—who wouldn't be, may I ask? But still, I yearn for higher ones.
                                                   BOY, 12, MICHIGAN

Sometimes I feel pressured into being always better than average. Every once in a while I just want to be below average.

GIRL, 12, KANSAS

I am waiting for the day I can face a blank page without fear, for the day I will stop running away from discovering myself and turn around to see what life's all about.   GIRL, 12, PENNSYLVANIA

The competition definitely gets harder when you get into higher grades, since everyone wants to be number one. I really have to give it my all, and more, to do well. For instance, in swimming, as my time got faster and I moved up, my competition moved up with me. I realize it's nice to win when you compete against others, but the most important part is beating yourself!   BOY, 12, MICHIGAN

Now that I'm in a gifted program, I push myself harder. I get mad at myself if I don't get good grades, and I wonder what will happen next.

BOY, 12, MICHIGAN

Question B: What Do Others—Adults or Friends— Expect From You, "A Gifted Child"?

EXPECTATIONS FROM ADULTS

My parents have said that even though I'm smart, I should put as much effort as I can into my work.   BOY, 7, CONNECTICUT

I sometimes feel that people expect me to be more polite and to be a good example to others.   GIRL, 7, NEW YORK

My teacher expects me to act differently. She expects me to check out harder books, to have better answers, and to do more.

BOY, 8, COLORADO

My mom thinks I should be able to hear better.

GIRL, 8, MAINE

One of my teachers expects me to explain answers. The others expect me to be able to answer questions the other kids can't answer.

GIRL, 9, ILLINOIS

My parents expect me to be more tolerant and understanding of those who are not as smart.   BOY, 9, ARIZONA

Sometimes when I act silly my mom says "Don't do that" or "Don't say that; you're too smart to do that." Sometimes, too, she says "Get harder and bigger books from the library." And I do (or don't).

GIRL, 9, OHIO

I feel like my teacher and family treat me the same. Even though I am gifted, people don't expect too much out of me.

GIRL, 9, CALIFORNIA

Others expect me to act more grown up, not playing games once in a while but studying every second.   GIRL, 10, CONNECTICUT

At school the teachers expect a lot but at home I feel like a regular boy.

BOY, 10, CONNECTICUT

Adults think I should act like a grown-up, not be any fun, and not play with anybody who's not in the gifted program.

BOY, 10, ILLINOIS

People expect so much just because I get *A*'s in everything except lunch.

GIRL, 10, NEW YORK

. . . I am expected to spell better.   BOY, 10, GEORGIA

When I do something bad they yell at me, but when I do something well they very seldom praise me . . . At the school I go to we have slippery rails and sometimes I slide down them and the regular class teacher gets mad. Just because I'm a gifted child, they expect me to act different.

BOY, 10, PENNSYLVANIA

Teachers expect me to be very organized, and I definitely am not!

GIRL, 10, ILLINOIS

I don't think my teachers, friends or parents expect me to act different. I just try to act like myself and try to do my best.

GIRL, 10, ILLINOIS

At home, no one expects me to act differently, they just expect me to act like any other kid. At school, they expect me to get better grades, speak better, and have better manners.   BOY, 10, CONNECTICUT

Some of my teachers say I should get all *A*'s and if I slack off they get very mad. They'll take me out in the hall to talk to me about it. I try to walk away, but instead, I usually stand there and don't listen. I may be smart, I may slack off, but I never got a *C* in my life.

BOY, 11, CONNECTICUT

In school, our P.E. teacher criticizes things our class does differently and says we are "gifted children who should be setting an example," as if a gifted child is perfect. *She* thinks we should be perfect.

GIRL, 11, VIRGINIA

If I fail a test (which is likely for an average seventh grader) I am looked at as if I should be hanged because that is not expected of a child of "my ability."   BOY, 11, CONNECTICUT

People usually expect me to be a "perfect example," an angel, or just plain ol' brilliant. If I bring home a math paper (or whatever) and I got a *C* or *D* on it, my Mom will say "Ellen! I'm surprised at you!" because she expects me to be the smart one of the family (and because I'm a teacher's daughter).   GIRL, 11, ILLINOIS

My parents are gently but surely pushing me, while my teachers literally make me do more work. This is a depressing subject. Let's get off it.

GIRL, 11, ILLINOIS

My teacher feels I should get *A*'s or *B*'s, and when I get a *C,* I can see she is disappointed. And my mother and father think I should do better in school if I get a *B*.   BOY, 12, NEW JERSEY

If a gifted student works hard on a project and gets an *A,* nothing is said of a positive nature. Fellow students think the teacher just takes a glance at the project, and as soon as she knows that it is yours, gives it an *A*. This is *not* true! Most teachers grade gifted students *harder*.

GIRL, 12, CONNECTICUT

If I ever misbehave at home my parents will say "And to think you are in a gifted program!" It can really start to bug me.

GIRL, 12, ILLINOIS

Because I have previously shown I am capable of getting good grades and understanding schoolwork, of course I am expected to "keep it up." Because of this, maybe, my teachers and parents expect me to grasp things more quickly and they have less patience with me if I don't. (But this often proves to be no great problem.)

GIRL, 12, WYOMING

At home, when I get in a fight with my brother, my parents will say "June, you're an intelligent girl, but you sure don't have much common sense." At school, teachers say "You should be a pleasure to work with, but you're sure not acting gifted today. I should be able to give you an assignment and you should have it done the next day."

GIRL, 12, CALIFORNIA

EXPECTATIONS FROM FRIENDS

If I go out to read a book on the playground, there is always someone to call me a bookworm. My teacher won't let me read on the playground because she says I read more words than I take steps.

BOY, 9, WYOMING

Nobody expects me to act differently if they take the time to get to know me.

BOY, 10, TEXAS

Lots of friends say "If you're so smart, I bet you can't do this." I really hate that. When people want me to do something that takes muscles, which has nothing to do with mental content, I get even angrier. It makes me mad!

BOY, 10, GEORGIA

At home my brother thinks I'm so smart that I am able to do all of his homework.
                                                                GIRL, 10, KANSAS

My friends think I should know everything. I hate that! They should treat me like everybody else.
                                                                GIRL, 10, CONNECTICUT

People expect me to be real stuck-up and sometimes treat me as if I am. I sometimes even exaggerate and tell people I make lower grades than I really do because I don't like to feel like an oddball.
                                                                BOY, 11, ALABAMA

When report cards come out everybody wants to know what I got. They expect me to have the best grades in the school.
                                                                BOY, 11, CONNECTICUT

Some people expect me to talk with big words, act right all the time, not be athletic, do things like staying inside all day reading. I do read, but not every second of my life.
                                                                BOY, 11, CONNECTICUT

I don't think any of my friends expect me to "act differently" because I think they can accept me for the way that I am.
                                                                GIRL, 11, PENNSYLVANIA

Some children at school expect me to be conceited or to brag about myself. I don't do this, though. For one thing, it makes the person who's bragging look like a fool, and secondly, I don't have to brag to feel proud of myself.
                                                                GIRL, 11, CALIFORNIA

My friends expect me to be a "goody two-shoes" because I'm in the gifted program, and they expect me to get straight $A+$'s. If I get an A instead, they say "You should do better."
                                                                GIRL, 11, CONNECTICUT

Question C: How Do Others React When You Make a Mistake? How Do *You* React When You Make a Mistake?

OTHERS' REACTIONS

When I make mistakes, my parents and uncle just tell me to start over, and my friends never say anything. But sometimes grownups say something really dumb like "Oh, Einstein, I thought you could do everything."

BOY, 6, VERMONT

A few people say "Alan, you should know everything!"

BOY, 7, MAINE

When I raise my hand and make a silly mistake, all the kids start to laugh at me and I start to turn red.   GIRL, 8, MAINE

When I make a mistake, I usually feel like disappearing because I know the kids in my class and my teachers expect more.

BOY, 9, WYOMING

People don't care if I make a mistake because everyone makes mistakes, even smart people like Einstein.   GIRL, 9, OHIO

Emily laughs. Beth doesn't do anything. I just correct it.

GIRL, 9, KANSAS

In class, nobody pays attention if I make a mistake. At home, my mother or father tries to show me how to do it right.

BOY, 10, CONNECTICUT

All the kids in school gasp in horror if I get below an 80%.

BOY, 10, CONNECTICUT

When I make a mistake everybody acts like I suddenly lost my brain. I feel very uncomfortable with this feeling.   BOY, 10, GEORGIA

People usually yell at me when I make a mistake and I start to cry or act like I ain't got a brain in my head.   GIRL, 11, GEORGIA

Here, people tease and taunt you if you make a mistake. I've had it happen to me before. People here support only those people with more muscle and less brain.   BOY, 11, CALIFORNIA

People compare how many mistakes I make and how many they make, and if I have more it just gives them a mental pat on the back. If I have fewer, they just think it's normal.   GIRL, 11, CONNECTICUT

People act the same as if someone else makes a mistake. But because I seldom get in trouble, if I do, my teachers always tell me how embarrassed I should be.   BOY, 11, GEORGIA

I think most people like to see me make mistakes because they get tired of me always getting good grades. They want to prove to themselves that I can't do everything perfect.   GIRL, 12, ILLINOIS

People laugh at me and sometimes a few of the teachers make a big deal out of a small mistake.   BOY, 12, CONNECTICUT

People are frequently *offended* when I make a mistake, or they pounce on me for making it. In return, I am inclined to be cynical, sarcastic, and embarrassed towards them.   GIRL, 13, WYOMING

Some kids at school think I have to be right all of the time. If I'm not, then there's something wrong, they think. That doesn't bother me, though; I just let it go by most of the time.   GIRL, 13, SOUTH DAKOTA

MY REACTIONS

When I make a mistake, some people are nice and help me find the answer. That makes me feel better about my mistakes. Some kids laugh and make fun of me. That makes me so angry that I want to punch them in the nose. But I don't do that because it isn't nice.

GIRL, 7, NEW YORK

I get very sad and mad and sometimes I want to rumple my papers so nobody has to see them! At the beginning of first grade (Now I'm in sccond) I didn't even want to do creative writing because I was afraid I wouldn't write exactly what the teacher wanted and she would say I made a mistake.

GIRL, 7, NEW YORK

. . . I feel embarrassed. Sometimes I feel so embarrassed I cry.

GIRL, 8, OHIO

When I make a mistakc I say in my mind DARN! and then I hit my desk or something.

GIRL, 9, ILLINOIS

When I make a mistake, people just correct me. I say a word wrong, sometimes, so my mom or dad just says the word right. I don't get all excited or anything.

GIRL, 9, CALIFORNIA

. . . I throw away my paper.

BOY, 10, CONNECTICUT

I don't think mistakes are big deals 'cause what counts is how hard you try.

GIRL, 10, CONNECTICUT

When I make a mistake others laugh, and so do I.

GIRL, 10, TEXAS

My parents tell me if I make a mistake it's OK and that everybody makes mistakes. But I get very frustrated. I know down deep that nobody is "pirfect" (ha! ha!) but I still get upset.

GIRL, 10, ILLINOIS

I just say to myself "I'll just try harder next time." I don't think it's such a big deal when I do something wrong.

GIRL, 10, CALIFORNIA

When I make a mistake I'm a little embarrassed but I'm not totally freaked out.

BOY, 10, CONNECTICUT

I try to hide all of my mistakes so I don't get teased.

GIRL, 10, CONNECTICUT

The way I react to making mistakes is I figure I did my best and everyone can make them. And by making mistakes I, and everyone else, can learn.

GIRL, 11, CALIFORNIA

I don't go by the mistakes that I make but rather the ones I solve or correct. I might breathe a brief "oops," but I don't make a big fuss over it, as I'm usually not too particular.   GIRL, 11, CONNECTICUT

When I make a mistake at first I laugh and try to figure out how I could have done it and then I get mad and make sure I don't do it again.

GIRL, 12, CALIFORNIA

I don't like it when I make mistakes, but most mistakes are either silly mistakes or caused by hurrying.   BOY, 12, NEW JERSEY

When nobody knows I've made a mistake I try to cover it up and make it look as if it *were* supposed to happen.   BOY, 12, VIRGINIA

. . . I turn red.   BOY, 13, CONNECTICUT

Question D: Do You Ever Do Anything "Just to Go Along With the Crowd"? Why or Why Not?

"YES"

Sometimes I do what my friends want me to do because some of the kids don't know as much about things as I do.   GIRL, 7, ILLINOIS

I was sick and my friend came over and wanted to play hide-n-seek and I said I felt better and I really didn't. It made me feel like I did something wrong. I felt dumb.   GIRL, 8, MAINE

. . . Yes, but most of the time I do what my conscience tells me to do.

GIRL, 9, OHIO

Sometimes I feel like I have to go along with the crowd because all my friends do. When I do something the way I want instead of the way my friends want, they get mad. I feel all alone when they get mad.

GIRL, 10, CALIFORNIA

Sometimes I do things so my friends who aren't in my gifted program will like me.   BOY, 10, GEORGIA

Sometimes I will go along with the crowd. You never know . . . they might be right!   BOY, 10, NEW YORK

Friends are often disappointed when I don't go along with them, but after a while they remember that everyone is free to be independent.

GIRL, 10, TEXAS

Sometimes I do go along just to fit in with the crowd. For instance, when my friends are playing something I'm really not interested in and I want to play with them, I play it.   GIRL, 10, CALIFORNIA

I do a lot of things to go along with the crowd, and when I decide to do things for myself, I very rarely come out ahead.

BOY, 10, TEXAS

Yes . . . because when I feel left out I feel like nobody likes me anymore.   BOY, 11, CALIFORNIA

I do do things to go along with the crowd—like asking questions I know the answers to just so they will treat me like one of them.

BOY, 11, ILLINOIS

Sometimes I will go along with the crowd, but I will always keep my own feelings inside.   GIRL, 11, GEORGIA

Last year in fifth grade I did something just to go along with the crowd. My parents didn't want me to, but I did. The situation was where no one liked this girl and they made fun of her. I was in with the group that did this, and now I wish I hadn't done it.   GIRL, 11, ILLINOIS

Sometimes I do things that my friends do even if we are bound to get into trouble. When I don't do what my friends want to do, they sometimes get mad.   GIRL, 11, OHIO

. . . If I decided I didn't want to do what my friends wanted me to do, I wouldn't have any friends.   GIRL, 12, CALIFORNIA

Sometimes I go down to arcades or the 7–11 just to show my friends I'm not all strange.   BOY, 12, NEW JERSEY

Sometimes I intentionally get a bad grade on a test so I won't look *too* smart. When I do what I want I am usually ignored.

BOY, 13, CONNECTICUT

Because I am gifted I can see that a lot of the things my peers do will appear silly or foolish to other people, and that some of the things they do could be potentially dangerous. Mostly, I try to stay out of those kinds of situations. However, in such a large junior high, I inevitably find myself in situations I don't like. When I don't go along with the group, people (my peers) often ridicule me or insult me, which hurts a lot, but I try not to let it bug me. In general, I would say I go along with the crowd except when I think it will hurt myself or others, physically or mentally.

GIRL, 13, WYOMING

"No"

Sometimes I do what my friends don't want me to do. Then my friends say they won't be my best friend. But I don't worry because tomorrow they're my friends.   BOY, 6, WYOMING

Sometimes when I do what I want to, like reading when I'm supposed to be doing something else, I get in trouble with my parents and teachers.

Other times I surprise them because I can do things well that they can't. My friends and I try to do a little what each other wants, then we're all happy.

GIRL, 7, NEW YORK

If I do something different from my friends, a few minutes later they will join me and say "Why didn't *I* think of this?"

GIRL, 8, ILLINOIS

I don't go along with the crowd because I think it's wrong to do something that I shouldn't do. If people call me chicken or other names, I just walk away.   GIRL, 9, CALIFORNIA

. . . very rarely! If my friends are playing a really stupid game, a lot of times I'll just tell them that the game doesn't excite me.

GIRL, 10, NEW YORK

. . . No, not really. For instance, I told my mom I wanted to let my hair grow long and she said "It's not in style, Joan." I said "I don't care, I do my own thing."   GIRL, 9, OHIO

Very often I persuade people to do what I want; usually I am a leader.

BOY, 9, CALIFORNIA

If I don't go along with the crowd, eventually I find something to do. At school, if I'm on bad terms with Tim, I join a game of bar tag, tire tag, or I just hop the tires.   BOY, 10, CALIFORNIA

I always try to be unique, and if someone asks me to do something just to be popular, I say "No way!"   GIRL, 10, TEXAS

When I do what I want to do instead of what they want me to do, they call me "poor sport." But I still do what I want anyway.

GIRL, 11, CALIFORNIA

I don't usually go along with the crowd because I don't usually have a crowd to go along with.   GIRL, 11, MAINE

Most of the time I stand up for the things I think are right. Sometimes my friends get mad at me because I don't do what they want, but I don't care because I know what I believe and nothing can change that.

BOY, 11, CALIFORNIA

Sometimes when I don't do what people want me to do they get angry with me, but I think that it's my life and I should get to do what *I* want because I'm a person, too.   GIRL, 11, CALIFORNIA

. . . I love to sing, dance and act so sometimes I'll start singing or I'll dance through the halls, or I'll jump in the air and land as a totally different character, such as Hamlet fencing with Laertes.

GIRL, 11, NEW YORK

I usually don't do anything to fit in with the crowd. There are my friends and other people who like me just the way I am so I don't try to be someone I'm not. My mom and dad taught me the difference between right and wrong, so I know how to make good judgments.

GIRL, 11, CALIFORNIA

. . . When I do something that others don't like and I stick by it and see it through, I feel good.   GIRL, 11, GEORGIA

I can't think of a time that I have "gone along with the crowd." Like in the case of designers and high heels and Izods, I don't have a single Izod, pair of designer jeans, or heels high enough to be accepted into the category. I do like some things that "the crowd" does, like playing video games, but I'm not a videoholic or anything. I don't like *some* things that the crowd does, like drugs and stuff, but none of that has come up yet in sixth grade. If it does, though, I feel I'm more likely to be an "outsider" to "the crowd."   GIRL, 11, VIRGINIA

I used to run with the group, but now I just try to be myself and do my best.   BOY, 12, OHIO

If I know I'm right, you'll be sure to know. If I don't do what other people want and they get mad, I feel that that's just their tough luck.

GIRL, 13, CONNECTICUT

CHAPTER 4

Schools That Work

Teachers encourage originality and creativity, stimulate your imagination, and care about you personally as well as schoolwise. They understand you're not perfect. They are friendly, they smile and make you feel good and happy. Teachers can *help.*

BOY, I I, MICHIGAN

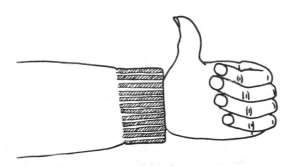

Children are the consumers of the commodity we call *education.* As such, they can be an important link in understanding and interpreting what goes on in our schools. If we take the time to ask, and then listen, we can learn much from their impressions and judgments.

This chapter is filled with positive comments from gifted children on those aspects of school that encourage learning to take place. First, students review their typical school days, and then they reveal what makes a school day perfect. In many instances the children provide proof that schools *are* succeeding and *are* benefiting students with high abilities. Some specific activities and methods that teachers use to help gifted children learn are highlighted by children in the second section of this chapter. A third section is a review of how children believe gifted programs should differ from other classes, in both content and style.

In the "Making Schools Better" section of this chapter, gifted children describe or list those teacher behaviors or school procedures in need of change. Most of the suggestions involve other-than-academic concerns, as teacher attitudes and reactions towards students come under scrutiny.

Lastly, the children detail those characteristics which make "a gifted teacher." It came as no surprise to me that personality ranks as high as ability as a prime quality of a gifted teacher.

Question A: Describe a "Typical" and a "Perfect" School Day.

TYPICAL

I take off my coat. We play a little bit. We sit down to do work. We go outside, if we have time. We go to lunch and then we rest. Sometimes we do something special. (I read to the class today!)

GIRL, 6, NEW YORK

I ride bikes, sit down, say pledge, do school work, read books with the teacher and read books by myself. I paint and do worksheets.

BOY, 6, NEW YORK

I have fun. Sometimes it's not fun, but I have to live with it.

BOY, 8, NEW YORK

In the morning we have math enrichment, and boy is it fun! Sometimes I come home with a problem and my mom can't even figure it out. Also, in school we get a lot of work and sometimes I have a lot of homework. Language is very challenging and isn't as easy as it sounds. At the present time we are learning about mythology. Every day in school I learn something new and exciting.   GIRL, 10, NEW YORK

I get on the bus at 6:30 and go through morning classes. At lunch I usually eat with Jane, Christine and Joey, then we all go outside. After school I like to go on long bike rides by myself just to think.

GIRL, 12, NEW YORK

PERFECT

Well, it would be getting straight A's and 100's. And also, the other kids wouldn't laugh at me and stuff. And I could go down to the media center and read.   GIRL, 8, NEW YORK

I would play in the classroom and pretend to be the teacher.

GIRL, 8, NEW YORK

. . . Everybody would be happy and no unfairness.

GIRL, 9, MICHIGAN

A perfect school day would be that it would be science day. We would study space, magnets and computers.   BOY, 10, NEW YORK

A perfect school day would be when the sun is shining, everyone is smiling, school work is easy and we don't have any homework.

GIRL, 10, NEW YORK

It would be a day that we have an awards assembly. I would *love* it if most of my friends would win awards that I could never win and they would not be mad if *I* won anything.   GIRL, 10, MICHIGAN

For a perfect day, all of the kids would be at school; the work would be challenging but fun; the lunch line would be short. At the end of the day I'd have no homework and the bus wouldn't be noisy.

GIRL, 10, MICHIGAN

A perfect school day would be having enough work to *fill* the day but not overflow it.   GIRL, 11, MICHIGAN

. . . If I learned to understand something new in most subjects.
                                                        BOY, 12, NEW YORK

A perfect school day would be when I could come to school and not be called "the smartest kid in the world." But even more important to me would be the day I could come to school and not hear anyone call anybody else a name of any sort. I realize that when that day comes, everyone will be sure of themselves and will not need to put other people down to gain confidence. To go through a day of school with everyone showing love to each other would be a perfect day for me.   BOY, 13, KENTUCKY

Question B: What Activities or Methods Do Teachers Use That Make Learning Worthwhile?

TEACHING ACTIVITIES

I enjoy going on trips so I can really see things. I also like to listen to records or watch a movie to learn things. It's kind of boring to just write our work on paper. I like to really see things and hear things and find out about things all by myself.   GIRL, 6, NEW YORK

I like learning by doing experiments and playing Mrs. Aaron's math and reading games. It is more fun than only memorizing and doing workbooks.
                                                        GIRL, 7, NEW YORK

I enjoy games that teach, for instance, Scamper. Scamper is a game that teaches children how to use their imaginations. The teacher reads things from a book and we try to imagine the things she says. Sometimes we draw pictures of what we saw in our imaginations. I like to draw the pictures and sometimes the stories are funny.   GIRL, 8, RHODE ISLAND

Before, I never used to like book reports, but ever since I did them with Mrs. Foster I've liked them. What she would do is have us either do a news report on it for the class or make costumes and act out our favorite part.

GIRL, 10, NEW YORK

. . . Current events. I follow up on something in the paper for a week. After that, I do a report, and each week I get to pick a new topic.

GIRL, 10, NEW YORK

My fifth grade teacher makes learning fun by doing an activity to help you learn. We have math sales, and that helps us with money while it's also lots of fun. In studying the Constitution we made bills and voted on them (now we can chew gum in class). For science, when we review for a test we play baseball, boys against girls. The teacher asks a question and if we get it right, that person goes to first base. We study while having fun. I think she is the best teacher I have ever had. GIRL, 10, CONNECTICUT

. . . One teacher I had in second grade taught us how to dissect a fish. That made me interested in being a surgeon.

BOY, 10, WEST GERMANY

We practice drawing with the right and left sides of the brain and we make learning centers. BOY, 11, ARKANSAS

I like making things, not watching things being made.

BOY, 11, GEORGIA

When I was in first and second grades my teachers recognized that I was gifted and decided to do something about it. What happened was I was getting very bored with my regular school work, so she decided that I would be able to do anything I wanted to do as long as I let her know what I was doing. Often I would end up doing some fourth or fifth grade math, reading, creative writing, and other things.

GIRL, 11, CONNECTICUT

. . . Field trips and having professionals, scientists, etc. come in and talk to the class. GIRL, 12, ILLINOIS

. . . Calligraphy, since now I can do more interesting things for cards. Besides, my handwriting needs all the help it can get!

GIRL, 12, GEORGIA

I really love brainstorming and writing stories and creative thinking books. I don't really like seeing movies and filmstrips—I like movies to entertain me, not teach me.   GIRL, 12, MINNESOTA

. . . Serious problems, like considering every little detail on how to make a town more hospitable.   BOY, 12, NEW YORK

I enjoy hands-on activities most of all, because they allow you to discover for yourself. Nothing is more strange than finding that all those dull words and figures in your texts actually mean something. Applied information, as I see it, is easier to remember.   GIRL, 12, CONNECTICUT

TEACHING METHODS

. . . calm, quiet teaching. I hate noise, and teachers when they yell.

GIRL, 7, NEW YORK

. . . Research. I like to find out new things.

GIRL, 9, NEW YORK

. . . To be taught in small groups.   BOY, 9, NEW YORK

I like the reports where we have to use other materials besides the encyclopedia to find the information.   GIRL, 10, MARYLAND

I like to do lots of creative projects and artwork *while* learning.

GIRL, 10, CONNECTICUT

My teacher in math sees if we know how to do our work, then she lets us work on our own if we know the other work.

GIRL, 10, CONNECTICUT

. . . Student participation, because student participation is fun, and when it's fun, kids remember it.   BOY, 10, NEW YORK

I like to be alone with the teacher and work directly with her.

GIRL, 10, NEW YORK

I enjoy filmstrips—they give you a chance to relax.

BOY, 10, NEW YORK

I like it when the teacher gives a good set of instructions and will set aside time to explain the topic if you don't understand it.

BOY, 11, CONNECTICUT

I like it when the teacher asks a child's opinion on something. That way, we get a say.   GIRL, 11, NEW YORK

I most enjoy teaching methods that are *not* logical, where I have a chance to talk or write creatively.   GIRL, 11, NEW YORK

I enjoy the teacher telling me I can do a project on anything.

BOY, 11, NEW YORK

I like working in groups because if you can't figure out the answer, someone else can.   BOY, 11, NEW YORK

I like my teacher to explain something that we are going to do ahead of time so that I can try to study it.   GIRL, 11, NEW YORK

I like a comical teacher that puts a lot of fun into learning because it makes me want to listen to everything he or she has to say.

BOY, 12, NEW YORK

I like to be able to ask a lot of questions. Sometimes the teacher will let us share information with the other classmates and let them learn a little from me.   BOY, 12, NEW YORK

I like when teachers let you figure things out on your own because you learn more that way.   GIRL, 12, NEW YORK

I like group activities the best. The reason I like them is because you can learn things on your own by doing research with your friends instead of taking notes while listening to a teacher lecture. Also, when you are in a group of kids you don't feel as shy about voicing your opinion or suggesting different ideas.   GIRL, 12, NEW YORK

Student participation and a non-serious method will both attract the learning interests of children better than the serious teacher who assigns more than he or she demonstrates.   BOY, 12, NEW YORK

I like classroom discussions. I like them because they give everyone a chance to exchange ideas openly.   BOY, 13, CONNECTICUT

Question C: What Should Be Done in a Gifted Program That Is Different From the Rest of a School's Classes?

We should play jumprope, learn to skip, learn to read books, learn to control ourselves, learn to model with clay, learn to sit in Indian style, learn to play indoor games, and learn to play with stuffed animals.
                                                          GIRL, 5, KANSAS

We should learn how many inches from the earth it is to the moon.
                                                          GIRL, 7, MAINE

. . . Special projects to learn about famous writers, artists and dancers would be interesting.   GIRL, 8, ILLINOIS

. Instead of just normal work we should have tests every day to see if we are improving. We should get to use materials on our level based on these tests. Every so often we should have a break so we could confer with the teacher regarding what we've done and what we will be doing.

GIRL, 8, CALIFORNIA

We should have harder work and less free time.

BOY, 9, WYOMING

We should have times where kids can study about a subject they want to learn about. We should have trips of special interest for the kids.

GIRL, 9, NEW YORK

There should be harder work given in gifted classrooms and more work given in less time. In other classes it is just the opposite—there is less hard work given in more time.   BOY, 9, CALIFORNIA

. . . Harder work, tough puzzles, or things that make us think.

BOY, 9, KANSAS

I think the gifted program should have more complex work instead of just speeded-up work. With the just speeded-up work, I understand it but it takes me longer because there is more. I would learn more if the work was more complex.   GIRL, IO, CALIFORNIA

We should use computers, play advanced games, and learn a lot about ourselves and how to deal with the fact that other people will always expect more out of us.   GIRL, IO, ARKANSAS

. . . Work on subjects that you will need to use in the next grade.

GIRL, IO, NEW YORK

. . . We should get more in-depth. We should have more freedom to choose the things we want to study.   BOY, IO, CONNECTICUT

There should be more creative writing and research—doing it! We should be able to work with kids as smart as we are and discuss things like our special problems with being smart.   BOY, IO, KANSAS

We should do like we did four years ago. In MGM (as it was called then) we learned sign language and braille. We didn't do all the other work like spelling, reading, math, English, handwriting, language, class discussion, science, and all the other "junk" we do now. MGM was just a great little one-hour class with puzzles, mind bogglers and other things.

BOY, 10, CALIFORNIA

Gifted programs should have special subjects like computers and archeology. I like to go into things that are more sophisticated and complicated.

BOY, 10, CONNECTICUT

I think gifted programs should have challenges, problems to solve, but most important, unstructured methods. For instance, classrooms don't always have to have desks, chairs and blackboards. Instead, they can have rugs, pillows and discussions.

GIRL, 10, MICHIGAN

It should be more difficult so teachers can see what we kids can do.

BOY, 10, NEW YORK

I think they should teach you about how to *use* your talents and gifts.

BOY, 10, ILLINOIS

In a gifted class, I think that the students should learn leadership activities and thinking skills.

GIRL, 11, OHIO

They should talk about what it is like to be gifted and how people who aren't very gifted feel. Also, talk about how you can help not-so-gifted children.

BOY, 11, GEORGIA

Parties! (No, just kidding.) They should have smarter teachers who could, with their own knowledge, extend on each subject. For example, math teachers could extend on boring decimals. Instead of doing the book, they could go into much more advanced problems.

GIRL, 11, ILLINOIS

I think that you should be able to make your own decisions and have an opinion in a gifted program. The school classes don't really give you these opportunities.

BOY, 11, CONNECTICUT

In a gifted program we should have more responsibilities and harder work (and that's just what our teacher gives us!). When you're in a gifted program, you have to use your head to figure out the work. But with more responsibilities and harder work, we often get more privileges.

GIRL, 11, CALIFORNIA

. . . Try to give the P.T.A. some advice on putting more things on the playground.   BOY, 11, CALIFORNIA

You can learn algebra and do different scientific experiments. You can also learn about computers and learn how to use the different buttons on a calculator.   GIRL, 11, PENNSYLVANIA

. . . Things that kids enjoy, not something that they hate or feel pressured by.   GIRL, 11, NEW YORK

If you like one subject in your normal class, during your gifted program you should learn more about that subject.   GIRL, 11, NEW YORK

Well, some kids may disagree, but I think we should have more work and harder work. Because what is the use of being gifted if there's nothing to be gifted about?   GIRL, 11, ILLINOIS

It should make gifted children feel like they're special. It makes *me* feel special. A gifted program needs a caring teacher that can make a child believe in himself or herself.   GIRL, 11, GEORGIA

A gifted program should have extra stimulating activities. Tailoring to each child would be necessary, too. The program should be fairly upbeat, helping the children like what they are better.

GIRL, 12, CONNECTICUT

I don't think we should do more of regular school work in a gifted program. We should go different places and see new things. The program should give us a chance to see and experience new things.

GIRL, 12, ILLINOIS

It means fun field trips and having a teacher who isn't so strict that the slightest wrong move warrants a parent/teacher conference.

BOY, 12, GEORGIA

They should gear the classes towards the individual children's strong and weak points.   GIRL, 12, ILLINOIS

We should get a chance to express ourselves, be ourselves, and find out who we are. And we do.   GIRL, 12, NEW YORK

We should discover and then learn instead of learn, then discover. What I mean is "experiment"—figure out things without a book telling you the answer.   GIRL, 12, ILLINOIS

Gifted programs should help kids like me relate to other kids. The programs should provide challenging word and logic problems, and encourage thinking skills. Gifted programs should not go along with the school curriculum, yet help us with our other schoolwork by providing a more extensive knowledge about it. Long-term independent projects are fine, as long as they don't interfere with homework. Most importantly, a gifted program should get kids off their duffs and start them thinking.

GIRL, 13, WYOMING

Question D: What Could Teachers Do to Make School a Better Place to Learn for Smart Students Like Yourself?

. . . Sometimes I wish I could do woodworking or anything that's unusual.   GIRL, 6, NEW YORK

. . . Have a nutritious meal, give us harder work, and don't let us have long recesses.   GIRL, 7, MICHIGAN

Let us do what we want when we want to.   GIRL, 7, MICHIGAN

Don't give us more homework than the others. Don't ask us to help everyone. Treat us like everyone else.   GIRL, 9, KENTUCKY

1. Make sure kids don't hit other kids.
2. Listen to what we say; don't holler as soon as we say one wrong word.
3. Make sure kids don't show off if they get 100.
4. Don't give so much work when the teacher knows we won't be there.
5. Give us short breaks if we have been writing a lot.
                                                BOY, 9, NEW YORK

1. More challenging problems.
2. More puzzling math.
3. To be more caring to some of the students who are not liked.
                                                BOY, 9, NEW YORK

1. I wish that teachers would keep smart workers from talkers.
2. When a teacher treats you like a baby, you act like a baby.
3. It would be nice if I was able to sit alone.
4. If the teacher would not interrupt your work.
5. If the books had some challenge.   BOY, 9, NEW YORK

Let us use our own ideas and help us when we need help. Be pleasant and don't yell, and treat everybody the same.   GIRL, 9, KENTUCKY

1. Have more reading time.
2. Start a foreign language sooner.
3. If you have decided what you want to be, you could start studying that occupation.   GIRL, 9, MICHIGAN

. . . Have a science lab table, a planetarium, and an invention room.
                                                BOY, 10, LOUISIANA

1. Have a special class for the smart kids and a few more classes for the rest of the people.
2. Don't spend the whole period explaining things—just get on with it.
3. Don't talk so loud when explaining so that we can't work while you're talking.
4. If we don't need work in an area, let us do something else.
                                                GIRL, 10, NEW YORK

1. Give us harder work in subjects where we're getting all *A*'s.
2. Don't go on and on about a subject kids already know.
3. Don't sit us near students who want to copy our papers.
4. Don't make us do an assignment that is too easy.
5. Give us extra time in the library.   GIRL, 11, MICHIGAN

1. Don't read people's work aloud to the class.
2. Don't say "there was only one *A* and so-and-so made it." (The class snickers.)
3. Don't always call on the smart students to answer harder questions.
4. Don't always expect the smarter people to make better grades than others.   GIRL, 11, KENTUCKY

1. Excelling is allowed.
2. If your work is done you can use the computers.
3. No dwelling on one subject.
4. If you do something right once, you won't have to do it again.
5. Have career lectures.   BOY, 11, MICHIGAN

I would like to be able to help other kids and I would like to help the teacher teach some of the things that need to be taught.

GIRL, 11, NEW YORK

1. Individualize the work a little so the student could work on things he/she had trouble with.
2. Combine the work with things the students enjoy doing.
3. Give kids more time to voice their opinions.
4. Encourage kids to get involved, to think, to create, to discover.

GIRL, 11, NEW YORK

1. Expect the best out of the students—no more, no less.
2. Banish all busy work.   GIRL, 12, KENTUCKY

Question E: We've Talked a Lot About Gifted Children, But What Makes a Teacher "A Gifted Teacher"?

A teacher who does different things is better than a teacher who does the same things every day.   BOY, 8, MASSACHUSETTS

When a teacher says nice things about me, gives me the privilege to do something, or says she enjoys helping me at any time, I think she's a gifted teacher for kindness.   BOY, 9, MASSACHUSETTS

She is capable of handling our problems and she has a good imagination to help us learn.   GIRL, 10, LOUISIANA

When they understand you and can give you help when you need it and don't say "Sit down and figure it out yourself," then teachers are gifted.   GIRL, 10, LOUISIANA

. . . Making complete plans and knowing what to do with them.   BOY, 10, LOUISIANA

I think a gifted teacher will challenge you and let the sky be your limit. When they go further than the book, it gets people more involved, especially if they bring in their own experiences. A good teacher won't overload you—you'll get breaks when you need them, and you get graded firmly but not too strictly.   BOY, 11, MICHIGAN

A gifted teacher:
—understands and respects gifted children
—encourages kids to set and achieve high goals
—goes into assignments deeper than the book
—writes compliments on your paper if you did a good job
—is responsible, efficient, and smart
—is loving and caring
                    BOYS AND GIRLS, 11 AND 12, MICHIGAN

A gifted teacher is someone who commands respect from the class. The best teacher I ever had was one who just had to say one word and the class would pay attention.   GIRL, 11, CONNECTICUT

A gifted teacher should have enough discipline to keep order in a class without being really strict. A gifted teacher should also have ways of teaching that not only the teacher but the majority of students like. She should also push students to their highest extent but know when they are not able to go further.   BOY, 11, WEST GERMANY

A gifted teacher opens your mind to help you with your life. She or he would help you by understanding your problems and by focusing on everybody as "gifted," for everyone really is.   BOY, 11, NEW JERSEY

A teacher is gifted when she knows what to do with each kid in her class. Like if she has a gifted kid and a kid who has a learning problem and she puts them in the same book, then she is not gifted, but if she puts each where they belong, then she is gifted.   GIRL, 11, NEBRASKA

. . . Being able to understand our feelings, ideas, and thoughts, and giving us the right amount of help with them.

GIRL, 11, LOUISIANA

. . . She treats me like a person, not a little kid! She smiles a lot and she understands me, lets me do projects that *I* want to do, no matter how hard they are.   GIRL, 12, NEW YORK

. . . She can joke on a younger child's level.   GIRL, 12, LOUISIANA

. . . When a teacher can be honest and when he or she can speak *to* the class and not *at* it.   GIRL, 12, VIRGINIA

CHAPTER 5

... When Schools Fail

All the time I just sat there,
Sat there
Waiting for something to happen.

My teachers should have ridden
with Jesse James
My teachers should have ridden
with Jesse James
For all the time they stole from me.

BOY, 11, MICHIGAN

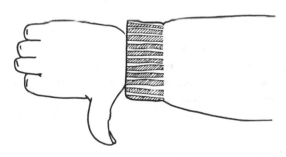

Despite the best of intentions and efforts, sometimes teachers disappoint their students. For this chapter, the gifted children pinpoint specific areas of weakness in teacher attitudes and behaviors.

In the first section, those dissatisfied with school review a typical school day. The next section is an elaboration on this dissatisfaction and lists specific teacher behaviors that gifted children dislike. Some comments here reveal frustration, others annoyance, and a few, disrespect or anger.

This chapter's third section is a set of responses to the question "Are you ever bored in school?'' Many students volunteer not only a ''yes'' or ''no,'' but comment further on why they respond as they do.

An observation: This chapter is a good degree shorter than the previous chapter, ''Schools That Work.'' The comparative length of these two chapters is in direct proportion to the positive/negative comments I received from gifted children regarding their education.

Question A: Describe Your "Typical" School Day.

We color and we do math. We read about Buffy and Mack. When we are doing work, we cannot get out of our seats except to throw something away. We have to be quiet. We do some more work, then we play, then we have lunch, then we do more work.   GIRL, 6, NEW YORK

It's a lot of work and I get frustrated. Sometimes I cry when I get home. I hate reading group.   GIRL, 8, NEW YORK

First, I do morning work. Second, I do my math. Third, I do my Head-ways book. Fourth, I go to the bathroom. Fifth, I have workshop. Sixth, I go to lunch. Next, I go to recess. Next, I do my reading book. Then I go home. We have only one time to play—that's at recess.
                                              BOY, 9, CONNECTICUT.

Oh what a bore to sit and listen,
To stuff we already know.
Do everything we've done and done again,
But we still must sit and listen.
Over and over read one more page
Oh bore, oh bore, oh bore.
Sometimes I feel if we do one more page
My head will explode with boreness rage
I wish I could get up right there and march right out the door.
                                              GIRL, 9, NEW YORK

. . . Forty-five minutes in math, forty-five minutes in language, then I spend four hours and thirty minutes more in a classroom.

BOY, 10, NEW YORK

I get in the classroom late, get lots of work, and take it all home.

GIRL, 10, NEW YORK

. . . most of the time it's just review, review, review.

GIRL, 10, MAINE

My typical school day is boring. I am lazy and do average. I try to do my work late and I still pass. I take advantage of being gifted.

GIRL, 11, NEW YORK

I spend thirty-two minutes in enrichment and the rest of the day in regular classes.

GIRL, 11, NEW YORK

I sit there pretending to be reading along when I'm really six pages ahead. Also, when I understand something and half the class doesn't, I have to sit there and listen.

GIRL, 11, ILLINOIS

On a regular day-to-day basis we have the same thing over and over.

BOY, 11, NEW YORK

First is math, which is very boring. Next, we have recess, then language (which I hate). Spelling is just before lunch. After lunch we have recess, then science. Finally, we have social studies and then get out of school.

GIRL, 11, CONNECTICUT

1. Sleep through reading.
2. Learn in my gifted program.
3. Read through health.
4. Look interested through math.
5. Pretend to take notes through social studies.
6. Throw up during lunch.

GIRL, 12, NEW YORK

. . . mostly boring, and when we first come in there's lots of work to do

and we have to work really hard. Sometimes my teacher yells at me because
I don't have my work done.   BOY, 12, NEW YORK

In a typical school day I whiz through my "extra" classes and plod
through the normal ones. Teachers repeat and "go over one more time"
and explain until their once-fresh ideas are almost meaningless. At times, I
try to block it out and then get reprimanded for not paying attention. Sometimes it's easier to just let the haze creep over my eyes and reply robot-like.
But it scares me—sometimes I feel like I'll never come back.
                                              GIRL, 12, CONNECTICUT

Usually, I come to school late, have to fumble at my locker, run up the
stairs and collapse into my seat. Then, it's off to the next class. It's pretty
monotonous, but it's a living.   GIRL, 13, NEW YORK

Some classes are boring, while others are slightly stimulating. I'm
planning to go to prep school so I don't have to sit through classes that are
below my level.   BOY, 13, NEW YORK

Question B: What Happens to You in School That Makes Learning More Difficult or Less Interesting?

Sometimes I get annoyed when teachers have to explain rules and things
over and over. So I help other people understand what they have to do.
Then we don't have to miss recess.   GIRL, 7, NEW YORK

My fourth grade teacher would give a test of ten questions. If I got five
out of ten wrong, I would get an "F−," but if a girl who was a little bit
below average got eight out of ten wrong, she would get an "A+."
                                              GIRL, 10, MAINE

The work isn't challenging a lot of times. Also, when I'm done with my
work, I have to wait for other people to finish (especially math).
                                              BOY, 10, CONNECTICUT

Last year I wasn't at school one day a week (my gifted program was in another school), so I didn't finish all my classwork. I would have finished but my teacher wouldn't let me bring anything home as homework. When my mother asked her about my grade, the teacher said that "if I was smart enough to go to another school I should be smart enough to keep up with my own classwork."

GIRL, 10, CONNECTICUT

I wish that teachers who use a lot of books would let you write in them. I don't like copying everything from my books onto papers, drawing perfect margins, making a heading, and writing everything exactly right. And . . . if you don't do it exactly the way you are supposed to, you get a "DNFD" which means you did not follow directions, and you keep doing it over and over until it is exactly the way the teacher wants it—even if you knew the material before you started.

GIRL, 11, CONNECTICUT

Once, in science, my teacher asked a question. I raised my hand to answer but he waved it away saying that he wanted someone other than me to answer because I had been answering too many questions already.

GIRL, 11, MICHIGAN

The teachers expect you to have the responsibility to get your work done, but if you ask them for it and they are busy and stuff, or if they are talking with one another, then the teacher'll say "Go in there and do your work!" What are you supposed to do?

GIRL, 11, CONNECTICUT

. . . If you say "I don't understand what's going on" they say "What's not to understand? You should know—you should have been listening." And you *were* listening but you just didn't understand and they won't explain to you. Then, you have a homework paper on that topic and you don't understand what it is all about and as a result you get a bad grade . . . and you want so badly to do well.

GIRL, 11, CONNECTICUT

. . . My math teacher expects me to know how to do very hard problems and won't explain them to me.

GIRL, 11, GEORGIA

Most teachers have tried to do something special, but in some grades teachers resented me because there was no one else working on my level. They had to think of extra programs and it was more work for them.

GIRL, 11, CONNECTICUT

. . . The teachers may only help those who are behind so their whole class is perfect.
                                                                    BOY, 11, MICHIGAN

If teachers call on people just because they raise their hand, and it's you, peers start talking about you. And if you *stop* raising your hand, who appreciates it? Certainly not the teacher, not the classmates—nobody. It's a relief when teachers have a variety of ways to choose people to answer questions.
                                                                    GIRL, 11, MICHIGAN

. . . I'm not saying that everything should be a production, but teachers should put something of themselves in their lessons.
                                                                    GIRL, 11, MICHIGAN

I hate it when teachers go into an interesting discussion and then decide that they haven't got time for it. It leaves me in total disappointment. If they didn't have time for it, then they shouldn't have brought it up in the first place!
                                                                    BOY, 11, MICHIGAN

I feel sometimes in school that I am playing a game with my teacher— that she is always trying to catch me off guard and that she wants to try to show off my faults. Whenever she plays this game, she always gets mad when I answer correct.
                                                                    GIRL, 12, CONNECTICUT

. . . I think I could be smarter in math, if they would give me a chance.
                                                                    BOY, 12, GEORGIA

The teachers often have me do extra things, like move desks or go get their coffee. I think this is indirectly a result of being smart, because I finish my homework first and am sitting there while the others are still writing.
                                                                    BOY, 12, OHIO

Most teachers are fair, but some teachers help slower kids get good grades more than brighter ones because they feel if slower kids get bad marks they won't try anymore. Work that would be a "D" for us might be an "A" for somebody else . . . It seems that some students don't work very hard but get better grades than some that do.
                                                                    GIRL, 12, CONNECTICUT

Our teachers treat us like we should know more and be smarter than the other kids. Sometimes it gets out of hand.   GIRL, 13, GEORGIA

There was one instance where I was having trouble finding the correct answer to a question in history. I asked the teacher for help and she refused, saying I was gifted so I should be capable of finding it. This makes me angry, and I've even thought about dropping out of my gifted program.

GIRL, 13, GEORGIA

Question C: Do You Ever Get Bored in School? If "No," Why Not, and If "Yes," What Do You Do to Relieve the Boredom?

"No"

No, I like school work very much and it gives me something to do all day.   GIRL, 9, ILLINOIS

School is never boring to me. I guess that's because I have a good teacher, or maybe because if I get bored I know my teacher will give me more work.   BOY, 9, CALIFORNIA

. . . I enjoy going to school and learning new things. I dislike play period because it means less time to learn the things I find interesting. But no, I never get bored.   GIRL, 10, NORTH CAROLINA

School is never boring to me because if I finish my work I always have something to do.   BOY, 10, WYOMING

School is Never, I repeat NEVER, EVER boring! It's almost a SIN to say school is boring!   GIRL, 10, ILLINOIS

School usually doesn't get boring for me, but it's also not my favorite way of spending six and one half hours. I enjoy seeing my friends and teachers, though. The teachers at our school are great and they are very nice.   GIRL, 11, CALIFORNIA

No, school isn't boring. My elementary school was, but junior high is a lot better.   BOY, 11, NEW YORK

I don't think school is boring at all. It's not that it's too difficult or anything, but I work hard for what I get—it doesn't just come naturally.
GIRL, 12, ILLINOIS

. . . Not since I entered seventh grade. In sixth you have the same teacher for six and one half hours. But in seventh you have nine different teachers—and all of them have so many likes and dislikes which are so *unalike*.   GIRL, 12, ILLINOIS

"YES"

. . . Most of the time, because I'd rather play than work.
GIRL, 6, NEW YORK

Most of my school work is easy for me. I've been reading since I was three years old and now I read library books for fourth graders and up.
BOY, 7, CONNECTICUT

School is boring when we review things I know by heart.
GIRL, 8, NEW YORK

School is boring in some subjects because I usually know the answers before the questions are even asked.   BOY, 9, WYOMING

I think school work (like writing words five times and putting them into sentences) is as boring as something can be—if you know how to do it already.   BOY, 10, KANSAS

We have to wait all day for the other kids and we do the same things day after day.   BOY, 10, PENNSYLVANIA

School is boring. Why? I imagine it's because either I know what is being talked about or I can't add anything to what the teacher is saying.
GIRL, 11, NEW YORK

. . . Yes, when the teacher talks too much.   GIRL, 11, NEW YORK

The only time that school was ever boring was in my sixth grade social studies class. I think I was bored because the teacher didn't give us any real challenges. I think, in a way, the teacher *made* it boring.
GIRL, 11, NEW YORK

Sometimes in the spring I get sick of the same old thing day after day after day.   GIRL, 11, NEW YORK

WHAT DO YOU DO TO RELIEVE THE BOREDOM?

I fiddle with my pencils or stare out the window.
GIRL, 8, NEW YORK

I sing to myself.   BOY, 8, NEW YORK

To entertain myself, I tap my feet.   GIRL, 8, OHIO

I always sit there and learn something because I don't want to be made fun of if I don't pay attention.   GIRL, 9, NEW YORK

What I usually do to get away from a lecture that I could easily give myself is take the bathroom pass even if I don't need it.
BOY, 9, WYOMING

. . . I imagine things.   GIRL, 9, NEW YORK

. . . I just let the day go by . . . it goes by SLOWLY, though.

GIRL, 9, NEW YORK

I pretend I'm home watching a rerun of a T.V. show. I remember the scenes in my head and watch the program.   GIRL, 10, NEW YORK

I read my favorite magazine.   BOY, 10, NEW YORK

I usually have something pretty on my desk to look at.

GIRL, 10, PENNSYLVANIA

To counteract the boredom, I joke around with the people next to me and get in trouble. That makes my recesses boring because then I have to stay inside.   BOY, 10, CONNECTICUT

I chew on my tongue to help pass the time.   GIRL, 10, MAINE

I am working to get more creative writing done and to try not to have to do things I already know how to do.   BOY, 10, KANSAS

. . . I listen but I think about something else.

GIRL, 10, NEW YORK

I sit and listen just in case I missed something the first time.

GIRL, 10, ILLINOIS

I tell jokes to myself.   BOY, 10, TEXAS

I read, or sometimes I think about home situations.

GIRL, 11, NEW YORK

To pass the time, I usually read or daydream or do something like this paper. I'm answering this question in the middle of a boring class, English.

GIRL, 11, ILLINOIS

Once I told the teacher I was bored and she even admitted that it was boring. Somehow, that made it seem more bearable.

GIRL, 11, CONNECTICUT

. . . I pretend I'm *not* bored.   GIRL, 11, NEW YORK

I go crazy, absolutely bonkers.   GIRL, 11, NEW YORK

Sometimes I finish my work early and I start to think about what's going to happen in the future.

                                                    GIRL, 10, NEW YORK

I sit without good posture.   GIRL, 11, NEW YORK

I like to write stories about my feelings and problems.

                                                    GIRL, 11, GEORGIA

When I get bored in math I pretend I am a computer *doing* the math. In social studies I pretend I am one of the people in that country.

                                                    GIRL, 11, NEW YORK

I just cope with it and find out what I can do for extra credit.

                                                    GIRL, 11, ILLINOIS

I listen as best I can and ask a lot of questions or I think about other things and half-listen so I can answer the teacher's questions.

                                                    GIRL, 11, NEW YORK

I try to walk around and hum to myself.   GIRL, 11, NEW YORK

. . . I'll pretend to be absorbed in a book.   BOY, 11, ILLINOIS

I look at all the pictures in the book real close to my face so they look like blurs, and then I pretend they're other things, like an elephant picture turns into a cloud or a lady or anything.   GIRL, 11, PUERTO RICO

Twice in social studies I fell asleep, but usually I would doodle and try to think of how I could learn more in the class even though it was boring. I've come up with a few ideas, like creative projects instead of doing plain old reports, and turning boring assignments into challenges.

GIRL, 11, NEW YORK

I usually write on my folders or look at the clock every now and then to see how long it takes our teacher to get through the part I already know.

GIRL, 12, ILLINOIS

I read a book or try to look interested. (I want to be an actress when I grow up, so this is good practice.)   GIRL, 12, NEW YORK

I look for a problem to tackle or else I try to make regular, everyday things into personal challenges.   GIRL, 12, NEW YORK

I was in math class last December. Our teacher had given us a long-term assignment and a week to do it in. I finished it on the first day. On the third day I started to get restless, so after counting the math problems left in the chapter, the pages in the chapter, the chapters in the book, and the pages I had already done, I was *bored!* As a last resort I passed a note saying "If you don't drop your book at 1:54 you are a purple cow." 1:54 came and everyone dropped their books . . . the teacher screamed "Who's responsible for this?" and the class, glad to get off the hook, said my name. I got into the trouble that I justly deserved.

I've found only one solution to boredom. Instead of rushing through work, take your time. Do something for extra credit. Then you won't get bored and the teacher won't assign you busy work.

GIRL, 12, CONNECTICUT

When school is boring I tell myself that school is my job and I have to do it.   GIRL, 12, NEW YORK

. . . I slip into a daze; I daydream. I dream I am a knight in shining armor, or in Ethiopia ruling hundreds of slaves.

BOY, 12, OHIO

. . . Talk to other bored students.   BOY, 12, NEW YORK

The teacher I have this year is quite a character. If he starts to get boring,

I just watch the way he moves and some of his gestures, which are kind of funny . . . this keeps me occupied.   GIRL, 12, CONNECTICUT

I throw down my thoughts on a piece of paper . . . I'm trying to write a book.   BOY, 12, CONNECTICUT

CHAPTER 6

Parents: A Helping Hand From Home

Be positive about your parents. Speaking for my parents, most of the time they are very helpful. I have a reason: they don't expect too much of me. But once in a while, they aren't angels. They can expect a little too much when they hear you're gifted. What I do is tell my parents what I think. Usually they understand. I feel they are proud of me and that encourages me to do even better.

GIRL, 11, MICHIGAN

The comments in this chapter reflect the opinions of gifted children on a topic they know very well: their parents. Responses to the first question revolve around children's reactions to any bragging their parents might do in connection with a youngster's academic abilities. Some children voice their opinions about sibling comparisons, while others comment on the proper time and place for parents to give compliments to their children.

In response to a question about parental expectations, some of the gifted children who respond think that only perfection is rewarded at home or that "my best" is sometimes not good enough. ("My mother likes me to improve all the time.") Of course, others reveal that their parents' expectations are fair or based on effort rather than performance (". . . if I try my best, that's good enough for them.")

Other sections of this chapter review those topics that are or *should* be discussed between bright children and their parents: the meaning of "giftedness," getting along with friends, and various other facts of life. Also, I asked the children to give parents some ideas for getting children interested in new topics or projects. Lastly, the children provide brief glimpses into the events and situations that make them happiest at home.

Question A: Do You Ever Catch Your Parents Bragging About Your Abilities or Comparing You to Your Brothers or Sisters? How Do You Feel About These Compliments or Comparisons?

BRAGGING OR COMPLIMENTING

When my parents praise me, I feel proud and important. Sometimes I feel like a wise man.   BOY, 8, KANSAS

When my mom or dad say I do well, I feel proud. But when my sister is in the room, I feel sad because no one says anything to her.

GIRL, 8, OHIO

My parents praise me for sharing. I always share my things with other kids, but I know some kids who don't. I don't think that's smart.

BOY, 8, NORTH CAROLINA

When I get praised by my parents, I thank them, then sneak away shyly.

GIRL, 9, ILLINOIS

I feel proud when someone compliments me. I feel proud because I'm gifted and I work hard to get their response.   GIRL, 9, CALIFORNIA

When grown-ups praise me around my peers, it makes me sound like I'm the only one with brains.   BOY, 10, PENNSYLVANIA

. . . I get a real good feeling inside me when I know I pleased them.

GIRL, 10, RHODE ISLAND

They don't praise me. They always say bad things. My mother sometimes thinks I should be perfect. She only praises my brother, just because
he's younger and more gifted than me when *I* was in second grade.

GIRL, 10, MAINE

When people give me compliments, lots of times I feel embarrassed because I don't know how to react. I don't know whether or not I will sound
conceited when I answer them. Lots of times all I do is grin and walk away.

GIRL, 10, CALIFORNIA

. . . I feel squashed, embarrassed.   GIRL, 10, PUERTO RICO

I feel good. I don't say anything like "I know I'm bright." I just say
"Thank you" and be done with it.   GIRL, 10, TEXAS

. . . I feel dumb. I hate when they praise me when one of my friends is
around.   GIRL, 10, CONNECTICUT

I feel very good all over. I feel like singing.   BOY, 10, TEXAS

I feel very good inside when my parents compliment me on something I
have done for school. But not always do they understand that the work
comes fairly easy for me.   GIRL, 10, ILLINOIS

My dad mostly embarrasses me by telling his friends that I'm real smart.
I never have the courage to tell him to stop it.

BOY, 11, NEW YORK

I don't like being complimented because I'm just using the abilities that
God gave me.   GIRL, 11, GEORGIA

. . . I feel embarrassed if I'm around other people, but if I'm by myself
I feel like someone cares.   GIRL, 11, OHIO

I like to know people like my work but I'd rather not be praised at all than
be embarrassed in front of my friends.   BOY, 11, MASSACHUSETTS

When my mother found out I was being put in a gifted program, she
called her friends to tell them. Her friends who have children my age told

their children and all my friends knew before I could tell them. I feel embarrassed telling my mother how I feel about this.

GIRL, 11, CONNECTICUT

. . . I don't mind except when my mother brings it into every conversation.

GIRL, 11, ALABAMA

I feel pretty good when I'm by myself and no one thinks I'm spoiled or a teacher's pet, but when I am with other people, I hate being told I am bright because they think I am a bigshot or something.

GIRL, 11, OHIO

It's nice when people compliment you, but parents *always* think their children are smart.

GIRL, 12, ILLINOIS

No one ever compliments me for being bright. All my mother has said is "I think, with your talent, you should aim for a good college—like Harvard or Yale, maybe." Other than that, no one mentions anything.

GIRL, 12, VIRGINIA

Too much praising would make anyone go crazy, but I don't mind it once in a while.

GIRL, 12, ILLINOIS

If my parents praise me for being bright in private it really makes me feel good. But when they do it in public it makes me feel a little uncomfortable, and I feel like people will call me "little goody two-shoes."

BOY, 12, VIRGINIA

Sometimes I don't know if I'm getting complimented or not because a lot of the things I do are the things my parents expect out of me. When I do get complimented I feel good—I feel like I've done a lot.

GIRL, 12, CALIFORNIA

I used to think "So what?", but now I really have learned to listen and appreciate compliments and then I tend to put forth more effort. Compliments kind of make me smile—like a hug. They sneak up and surround you to protect you from anything bad.

GIRL, 12, KANSAS

. . . I have a feeling of personal pride, yet if it's done in the classroom, I feel I've been kicked in the teeth because of some of the comments that are made. However, I have learned to accept my gift *as* a gift and not as an unwanted burden.   GIRL, 13, CONNECTICUT

COMPARISONS

My mom and dad and other people usually compare me and my sister. They do it by looking at our report cards. And if my sister has a *one* (meaning excellent) and I have a *two* (meaning good) they yell at me, and I don't like that. They make me feel bad.   GIRL, 9, NEW JERSEY

I feel my mother thinks my brother's better at games and sports. It makes me feel I'm always the second best at things.   BOY, 9, NEW YORK

Sometimes they compare my brother and me and it makes me feel bad because my brother is older than I am and he does things better.
                                                    GIRL, 9, NEW YORK

I have been compared with my sister before. My grandparents sometimes say to my parents when I'm sitting right there "My, Martha can do gymnastics so well, why can't Barbara?" That really gets me mad.
                                                    GIRL, 9, NEW YORK

Sometimes my parents say "Your sister did this and that when she was little, so why can't you?" I feel like saying it's because I'm a different person than my sister!   GIRL, 9, ALASKA

I'm compared, by both my parents *and* my brothers. And it makes me feel cruddy.   GIRL, 9, MASSACHUSETTS

My mother says that I am smarter than my brother. It makes me feel weird. I think he should be smarter than me because he is older.
                                                BOY, 10, WEST GERMANY

My parents compare me with my sister a lot. They compare me by saying things like "See how quiet your sister is?" or "You got a *B* on your report card and your sister got all *A*'s and *A*+'s." It makes me feel like they're talking about me as if I'm not even there.   GIRL, 10, NEW JERSEY

My mom *and* dad say that when my older brother was my age he was only about ¾ as smart as me.   GIRL, 10, NEW JERSEY

I am almost never compared to my brother but when I am, I get mad.
                                                          BOY, 10, MICHIGAN

My brother and I are not usually compared because we each have our own special gifts.   GIRL, 11, NEW YORK

My step-dad compares me to my older step-brothers which makes me feel he expects more out of *me*. . . . Which means they get to do a lot more with Dad than I do (partially because they're boys and I'm not).
                                                          GIRL, 11, MICHIGAN

My gramma compares me to others. It makes me feel uncomfortable (even though I'm not the one who is on the side that's supposed to be the one who is not as good as others). I don't think comparing is fair.
                                                          GIRL, 11, MASSACHUSETTS

I am sometimes compared to my smaller brother by my parents. It makes me feel very smart and very capable. It also brings back memories of when I was younger.   BOY, 11, WEST GERMANY

My sister and I are not compared very often because we have different interests and do different things.   GIRL, 11, MICHIGAN

I'm compared to my brothers and sisters by my father. It makes me feel like I have to do everything they did—like win spelling bees and science awards.   GIRL, 12, KENTUCKY

Question B: What Have Your Parents Said to You About Being Gifted? What Expectations Do Your Parents Have of You Because of Your Abilities?

"WHAT THEY'VE SAID"

. . . They told me that being smart makes other kids nervous.

BOY, 6, MASSACHUSETTS

My parents say that they are glad I'm smart because I can help the world.

BOY, 7, NEW YORK

My parents have talked to me about being smart lots of times. They said I should use my head for doing good and right things. They said I shouldn't be mean to others and that I shouldn't make fun of others because they're not as smart as me. And, don't make fun of people and call them stupid because I wouldn't want them to do that to me.

GIRL, 9, MASSACHUSETTS

My parents have very much talked to me about being smart. They will say something like "Do you realize the fact that you are gifted?" One time, our talk lasted an hour.   GIRL, 9, NEW YORK

. . . They say I am as smart as a computer.   BOY, 9, NEW YORK

My parents never talk to me about being smart. I usually don't have any time to talk to my mom. I have to go to practice my piano or go to gymnastics. Sometimes, I just want to play.   GIRL, 9, KENTUCKY

My mom talks to me when I do not want to use my full abilities. For instance, when I want to get out of something because the work is too tough.

BOY, 10, NEW YORK

. . . They say I'm a very lucky girl because I can do what I want when I'm older.   GIRL, 10, NEW YORK

They know I am bright but we don't need to talk about it because there is no problem.   GIRL, 10, NEW YORK

I have gotten three papers this year that had to be signed by my parents because my grade was below 70. My parents say, "For someone with your smarts, that shouldn't have happened."   GIRL, 11, MASSACHUSETTS

My parents say that everyone is talented in some areas and I should be very careful if the subject of the talented and gifted program ever comes up so I don't happen to cause hard feelings on the side of someone who is talented in other areas.   BOY, 11, WEST GERMANY

My parents haven't ever talked to me about the fact that I am smart.

GIRL, 11, NEW YORK

My mother had a long talk with me about it and she told me it was great to be smart but she also told me not to be snobby about it.

GIRL, 11, ALASKA

My mom says that I am smart and that I shouldn't try to hide it because it is a fact. She also says I was lucky to be born smart, and now that I have this gift I should use it to the full extent of my abilities.

GIRL, 11, NEBRASKA

My parents said that because I'm smart I could be anything I want to be when I grow up, from a garbage collector to the President.

BOY, 11, MICHIGAN

My parents have helped me feel OK about being intelligent. This gave me self-confidence.   BOY, 11, WEST GERMANY

My mother has talked to me about my intelligence and the one thing I remember her telling me was not to think I'm better than anyone else, because I'm not.   GIRL, 11, NEW YORK

My parents haven't really talked to me about being smart. However, sometimes when I'm not doing anything my mom'll say "Donna, you're a bright girl, why don't you do something to advance?"

GIRL, 11, NEW YORK

. . . They ask me how I feel when other kids tease me about being smart. They give me support.   GIRL, 11, KENTUCKY

My parents have said that I must push myself and set high goals and reach them.   GIRL, 11, MICHIGAN

My parents never talk to me about being smart. Most of the time I get the feeling they just don't care.   GIRL, 12, KENTUCKY

My parents talked to me about being smart when I was getting ready to skip fourth grade. They told me that I was gifted and they asked me if I thought I could handle skipping.   GIRL, 12, KENTUCKY

My parents have many times talked to me about my special talents. I seem to accomplish in everything I do and they realize this. They talk with me about many things, they encourage me and they love me. My parents and I have a very good relationship. We feel that my special talents have been given to me by God, and I realize that because of this blessing there is something special about my life.   BOY, 13, KENTUCKY

"What They Expect"

At home my parents expect me to do things perfectly. For example, when I ask how to spell a word, they ask "Why are you in the gifted program if you can't spell?"   GIRL, 8, ILLINOIS

They have said to me that I am the cutest and smartest kid in the world, but only if I don't do anything wrong. They get angry if I make too many mistakes.   BOY, 9, NEW YORK

. . . My mother likes me to improve all the time.

BOY, 9, NEW YORK

My dad sometimes expects me to do better. In Cub Scouts, I'm over-loaded. If I do ten push-ups, thirty sit-ups, and make the fifty-yard dash in the required time, he doesn't accept it as good. (It's usually the fifty-yard dash that does me in.)   BOY, 10, CALIFORNIA

I think that my parents want me to do better at home because I'm gifted. I think they expect too much.   BOY, 10, KANSAS

My parents don't care that much about my grades—it's the effort that counts to them.   GIRL, 10, CALIFORNIA

My parents only expect me to be a normal, average girl who can add little interesting comments into the conversation.
                    GIRL, 10, CONNECTICUT

Sometimes when I get B's they get angry, but otherwise they just feel proud of me.   GIRL, 11, CONNECTICUT

Parents give you the needed support and put you back on your feet when you're down. My parents don't make a big hullabaloo when I'm not totally an A student. They realize we all have our bad days.
                    BOY, 11, MICHIGAN

My mother expects me to be smarter than I was before I was labeled "gifted."   GIRL, 12, CALIFORNIA

I think at home I am expected to be very responsible and I also think my parents get most upset when I bug my brothers. They feel that I am old enough to leave them alone, and they say "If you're supposed to be so smart and gifted, why don't you act like it?" They really expect me to act grown-up even though I'm still a kid.   GIRL, 12, ILLINOIS

I always try to do my best, but for my mom, that isn't enough.
                    GIRL, 12, CALIFORNIA

Sometimes my parents say I should have more sense because I'm in a gifted program.   GIRL, 12, CONNECTICUT

My parents congratulate me when I get an A, but if I get a B or lower, they say that if I tried my best, that's good enough for them.
                    GIRL, 12, CONNECTICUT

Everyone in my family has an IQ over 130. My mother's is 160-some-
thing. We all understand that "bright" people have problems, too.

GIRL, 13, LOUISIANA

Question C: What Have Your Parents Done to Get You Interested in New Topics, and What *Haven't* They Discussed With You That You Believe They Should?

"GETTING ME INTERESTED"

. . . They forced me into it.   GIRL, 7, MICHIGAN

My parents have put me in classes that they thought I would like. Also,
they take me different places to see things.   GIRL, 8, MICHIGAN

They have cleared their throats and just started talking.

GIRL, 8, NEW YORK

. . . Nothing; they don't have to.   BOY, 8, NEW YORK

They have challenged me to do things that I don't even like to do, just to
prove that I don't really know the good from the bad . . . and again, they
prove themselves right.   BOY, 8, NEW YORK

My parents buy me lots of books, especially books about things I am interested in, like baseball and Greek myths.   BOY, 9, NEW YORK

My mother and my father got me interested in nature and science because
my parents and I go on nature hikes and trails. Learning about nature got a
lot of requirements done on my Girl Scout badges, too.

GIRL, 9, NEW YORK

My father teaches me everything in math before I even know what he is talking about. It helps me to really get interested in new topics.

GIRL, 10, MASSACHUSETTS

My mother took me to the Metropolitan Museum to see the Egyptian exhibition so that I got interested in history.   BOY, 10, NEW YORK

My parents get me interested in new topics by encouraging me to read different kinds of books. My parents also insist I join things in and out of school to keep busy.   GIRL, 11, NEW YORK

My family has valued education and religion for many generations. When I was small I had many questions to ask about both, and my parents were happy to answer. By asking those questions and getting them answered, I gradually have grown a passion for learning, and all because my parents were there when I needed them.   GIRL, 11, MICHIGAN

My parents, each in their own ways, let me be independent. I get responsibilities that I can handle, and I'm very thankful. They treat me like an adult, talk to me like an adult, and trust me like an adult. They let me try art, literature and other special things. And they listen to me—it helps so much that they listen. They let me make decisions for myself, even if they think it's not a good idea. What's more, they're very patient—they help, but they don't push. Most important, they respect me.

GIRL, 11, MICHIGAN

They have given me responsibility so that I can handle it wisely. They have given me plenty of artistic things, which started my creativity very well.   BOY, 11, MASSACHUSETTS

When my mom wanted me to take ballet, she kept talking about it and then it started to make me curious. She started me in it and now I'm doing well.   GIRL, 11, MASSACHUSETTS

. . . They set an influence on me to try to read, and now I'm in the highest reading group.   GIRL, 11, MASSACHUSETTS

My parents get me interested in new topics by talking a lot about them and telling me a lot about the good points and the bad points of the topics.

GIRL, II, NEW YORK

When I was in kindergarten, they showed me how to say the alphabet and count and add. Now they try to help me study and do book reports.

BOY, I2, NEW JERSEY

. . . If I'm interested in something, they try to find someone who will teach me well!   GIRL, I2, NEW YORK

We often visit historical places and I am encouraged to read books or magazines, which helps me to learn about many new and different topics.

GIRL, I2, MICHIGAN

"TOPICS NOT DISCUSSED"

I think they should talk to me more about how they think I am doing in school. It is important to me because then I would know how they feel about it.   GIRL, 8, MICHIGAN

Sex. Because if they don't tell me, how am I supposed to learn?

GIRL, 9, MICHIGAN

They talk *about* me and where I should go and I think they should talk *to* me to see if I agree on it.   BOY, 9, NEW YORK

They hardly ask me about my school—but I think they should.

GIRL, 9, MAINE

My parents don't talk to me enough about managing money—how to live on a certain budget. I need to learn this so when I want to go to college I'll have the money.   GIRL, I0, NEW YORK

. . . The real reason my parents got separated, because I need to know.

BOY, I0, NEW YORK

. . . Boy-girl relationships, because I'm about ready to have one.

                                                    BOY, IO, MICHIGAN

My parents don't talk enough about growing up. I like to know what's going to happen to me before it does. Some parents don't talk about things like that, but I think they should. Kids need to know when they are growing up.   GIRL, IO, KENTUCKY

There aren't many secrets in the family, except for surprises. Otherwise, most troubles of the family are talked about openly.

                                                    GIRL, II, NEW YORK

My parents talk about mostly everything I want to know. Sometimes they don't have the answers, though, to all my questions.

                                                    GIRL, II, NEW YORK

My parents discuss almost everything with me, and what they don't, I usually don't want to know about.   BOY, II, NEW YORK

If I say "My class had a test today," all they do is say "That's nice" and change the subject. One time I had a big report due. I got it back and got a good grade on it. My parents know how important it is to me to get good grades on things—but all they said this time was "Uh-huh."

                                                    GIRL, I2, NEW YORK

Question D: Who or What Makes You Happiest at Home?

. . . When we have all the time in the world.   BOY, 8, NEW YORK

When I cuddle with my mother.   GIRL, 8, NEW YORK

When I am alone with one of my parents and we are having a nice, quiet time.   GIRL, 9, OHIO

When my father takes time with me on things I want to learn. He shows me he loves me, tries to teach me.

BOY, 9, MASSACHUSETTS

When my older brother and sisters recognize me as an equal.

GIRL, 10, NEW YORK

. . . My mom is a counselor and she is sensitive and listens to my problems. She is there any time I need her.

GIRL, 10, LOUISIANA

When my grandma, grandpa, aunt and uncle come over and we all laugh, tell each other our latest jokes, and eat dinner.

GIRL, 10, MICHIGAN

I'm probably happiest at home when I have a bad day at school and I walk inside my home and my mom gives me a kiss promptly.

BOY, 11, LOUISIANA

My father always says that working hard will help me when I grow up and will help me with my career. My dad spends a lot of time with me on the weekends, playing games and sports with me. He coaches basketball and baseball and has taught me all the sports I know how to play. I have learned how to make friends easily. Even though I am bright, he has made me feel like a "regular American kid."

BOY, 11, NEW JERSEY

I am the happiest at home at dinner time because I get to find out how each other's day went along. I talk with my family to see what they did at school, work or home.

GIRL, 11, NEW YORK

My father helps me at home because he understands me and how I feel. But he's not the only one who has helped me. As a matter of fact, even the most minor person in my life has taught me a valuable lesson on adjusting to life, and now, I feel much better about myself.

BOY, 11, NEW JERSEY

I'm happiest at home when our whole family is sitting around the quartz heater together, and when we are playing ping-pong.

BOY, 11, MINNESOTA

My favorite thing was when I got beat up by the un-gifted kids in my old school, because that was why my mom decided I could go to an all-gifted private school.   GIRL, 12, MICHIGAN

CHAPTER 7

Future Goals, Future Quests

KIDS AND KITES

Kites fly,
but they need an anchor.
Kids roam,
but they need a home.
If a kite loses its anchor,
it falls.
If a child loses his home,
he declines.
As a kite goes higher and higher
you give it more string.
As a child grows older and older
you give him more freedom.
But here
the similarity ends;
For kites,
even with the most string imaginable,
crash sooner or later.
But kids,
(if they are old enough),
adjust safely
and create new homes.

BOY, II, CONNECTICUT

Even the youngest among us looks to the future for the possibilities it holds. As adults, we consider our jobs and our families, and we play with dreams and goals that we hope will be reached. Children, too, have wishes—different more in degree than kind, perhaps, from those of adults.

This chapter is a sampling of those wishes that gifted children have for themselves in terms of both school and later life. I asked the children to review what they would like to learn about but, as of yet, had not had the time to explore. Also, I asked them to look towards their "future plans," which most of the children interpreted as meaning going to college, raising a family, and choosing a career. As you shall read, the children will seek their happiness as most of us do: through a career, a family, and a good measure of self-satisfaction.

Question A: What Would You Like to Learn About That, Up Until Now, You Haven't Had Time to Explore?

I would want to study stars. Sometime, I want to sleep in a tent and in the night go outside and try to find the Big Dipper and other constellations.

GIRL, 8, NEW YORK

This isn't a school subject, but I'd like to study about *people* so that if they have problems, I can help them.   GIRL, 9, MASSACHUSETTS

I would like to learn about John Alden because I know one of his descendants.   GIRL, 9, CONNECTICUT

. . . Amelia Earhart. I want to find out where she crashed and how. I've always liked her, but I'm not sure why.   GIRL, 9, KENTUCKY

I think I would like to learn about Easter Island because I like archeology.   GIRL, 9, KENTUCKY

I would like to learn how to make a book—binding, covering, writing, the whole thing. I plan to write books and if I learn how to do these things, I could give someone a book that I had made all by myself.

GIRL, 10, KENTUCKY

I would like to study about computers and work with them because some-day everything will be run by a computer and so I would like to work with them now so that I have a little head start.   GIRL, IO, NEW YORK

I'd like to learn about where we will live if the earth blows up, and how we would get there.   GIRL, IO, NEW YORK

I would like to learn about and work with chemicals. It is neat how acids can burn holes in things.   GIRL, IO, MICHIGAN

I would like to learn about space travel because it seems to be the ulti-mate thing these days.   BOY, IO, MASSACHUSETTS

I would like to study fossils because they're so interesting. For instance, sometimes worms will leave marks in rocks and it's kind of weird because worms don't seem heavy enough to leave trails. I like fossils because they're like preservatives and they save bones and tracks made a long time ago.   GIRL, IO, NEW YORK

. . . Boys, because I'm smart and always have been and because of that they tease me.   GIRL, I I, MASSACHUSETTS

I'd like to learn about records. So I'd know how sound gets into the grooves and is able to come out in the form of music.
                    GIRL, I I, MASSACHUSETTS

. . . I have always wanted to know how the eye works—how it gives you a picture.   GIRL, I I, MICHIGAN

I think I would like to study more about prehistoric times. I'm interested in how the dinosaurs suddenly "disappeared." There are a few very possi-ble explanations, but there really isn't a lot of proof that any are true.
                    GIRL, I I, NEW YORK

I would like to learn more about Catholics. My mother is Methodist, so that's our religion. But I don't know much info on other religions so I want to have more.   GIRL, I I, LOUISIANA

. . . Medieval weaponry, because that way I will know what a weapon looks like when I play *Dungeons and Dragons*.

BOY, 11, MINNESOTA

I'd like to study how computers work. My dad is an electrical engineer and fixes things in his workshop that deal with wires, and I think it would be neat to know how a computer works.   GIRL, 12, NEW YORK

I would like to study about animal behavior because I *love* animals and I would like to be with them all my life. I would also like to know how to help them not become extinct.   GIRL, 12, NEW YORK

I would like to study deeper into the area of counseling because I am a person who cares very much for the people around me. I understand many problems and enjoy telling people what they ought to do to resolve a problem. This gives me much more satisfaction than anything else I could possibly do.   BOY, 13, KENTUCKY

Question B: What Are Your Future Plans?

. . . A lot of things—go to college, ride horses, learn about people, and fly to the stars.   GIRL, 6, MASSACHUSETTS

I want to be a mom and a waitress and a lawyer.

GIRL, 6, MICHIGAN

I had two plans for my career. One was to be a dancer and the other was to be a teacher. So I decided to be a dance teacher.

GIRL, 8, NEW YORK

I want to go to college and be a half-time ski instructor.

GIRL, 8, MICHIGAN

. . . I sort of want people to know me when I die.

BOY, 8, NEW YORK

To either teach children that are mentally handicapped or (most probably) go to hospitals and dance and sing for them.

GIRL, 9, MASSACHUSETTS

I would like to be a dancing teacher, and a waitress when I have the days off.

GIRL, 9, MASSACHUSETTS

I would like to be a veterinarian because I love pets and if they were sick or needed shots I would be glad to help them. I know how it feels to have a pet die or run away. One cat of mine went hunting one day and never came back.

GIRL, 9, NEW YORK

My future plans are to grow up and try to work hard to be a dentist. I'd like to be a dentist because it seems a little challenging to find out if anybody has cavities. I wouldn't charge much of a fee. I'm thinking about retiring at 54.

BOY, 9, NEW YORK

I would like to teach other kids and grown-ups what I have learned in my life so that they can become teachers and teach other people their wisdom.

BOY, 10, NEW YORK

I plan to finish college and get a teaching degree and teach kids with problems, or a gifted class. After I retire, I plan to write stories. (I love to write!) Those are only my plans if I don't succeed in my first wish: I want to be the first woman President.

GIRL, 10, KENTUCKY

I want to go to medical school to be a veterinarian. For one reason, I love animals, and for another, they make good money!

GIRL, 10, NEW YORK

I plan to be a doctor. I think I'll get married someday and maybe have a few kids. In my spare time, I'll write poetry.

GIRL, 10, MICHIGAN

I don't want to be noticed as being smart. I just want to be a regular housewife because I don't think it's fair that just because I'm smart I have to be a scientist or something.

GIRL, 10, NEW YORK

I want to be a surgeon because I want to learn how the insides of people work.   BOY, 10, WEST GERMANY

I will go to high school, and for college, I will go to the University of Florida. Then I'll become a real estator or get involved in computers. I might get married and then go into retirement and Medicare.

                                                        BOY, 10, KENTUCKY

My future plans are to go to Penn State and play either football or baseball or both. And whichever one I like best will be my career. I will also take up some kind of back-up career.   BOY, 10, ALASKA

I would like to become a professor or a scientist. I think I would like to create things that would help the world. It would also be interesting to pass on the information I have learned to others.   BOY, 10, NEW YORK

1. Go to college and graduate school.
2. Get married and find a well-paying job.
3. Help my children to become good people.

                                                    GIRL, 10, NEW YORK

I'd like to be an actress, singer, physical therapist or teacher. When I'm about 20, I plan to pursue my career (whatever it is) and find the perfect place to live and work. When I retire I would like to travel around to China, Africa, and other places I would enjoy seeing. After that, I would like to find a nice, cozy house to live in in Switzerland.

                                                    GIRL, 10, MICHIGAN

I want to grow up to be a professional ballet dancer. I want to do archeology in my spare time. I plan to be single and travel around the world.

                                                    GIRL, 11, MICHIGAN

I would like to be an Egyptologist or doctor. I *really* couldn't see myself as a secretary.   GIRL, 11, MASSACHUSETTS

I might be a child psychiatrist. I am very interested in exploring the mind and I also want to help other people (which will make me feel more useful to the world).   GIRL, 11, LOUISIANA

When I grow up I'll have a mustache, a Fiat, and I'll be a naturalist and I'll adopt twins.   BOY, 11, MICHIGAN

I expect to go to college, but I have no career plans now. I don't have any plans because I have too many things I like to do and I am good at. Some people are only good at one special thing and I am good in many areas.

BOY, 11, WEST GERMANY

I plan to be an architect. I'm already drawing plans and in fact, my best plans are for my future house. It is underground. People probably think it's for art, because it's 4,500 square feet and it would cost $272,000. I also plan to have a sailboat on the ocean (*it* has a rather large price itself).

BOY, 11, LOUISIANA

. . . To become a pro football player and not to sit on the bench all the time.   BOY, 11, LOUISIANA

Most kids want to be doctors, lawyers, or artists, but I want to be an athlete of some kind.   BOY, 11, GEORGIA

I'm not sure. But I really would love to be a detective. Everybody laughs when I tell them this, but I am interested in that subject and I just might grow up and make it work.   GIRL, 12, MICHIGAN

My future plans were to be a teacher, but my mom said that with my brains I should be something else.   GIRL, 12, MICHIGAN

In our school we have what's called "group guidance." This is a course that helps you to choose a career and set values for what you think is most important so you will choose a good career for you and your lifestyle. Ever since I was little I've wanted to be a lawyer because I think that some things that are in laws should be changed. I also plan to achieve high in my high school so I will be able to attend Harvard College and Law School. In the way, way future, I plan to become President of the U.S. or a Senator or Congressman so I can change things that aren't fair to someone or a group of people.   GIRL, 13, NEW JERSEY

CHAPTER 8

Letters: Learning From Others

Dear Friend,
Being in a gifted program
May not be like you think.
Some kids think you're great
and some kids think you stink.
It's not free time; it is work,
But whatever you choose to do,
It's a nice, polite environment
With teachers to help you.
Your peer group may pressure you,
So choose who you want to be.
Just remember: everyone is unique—
You are you and I am me.

BOY, 11, CONNECTICUT

Different from the others, this chapter is not based on a particular theme of "parents" or "teachers" or "friends." Rather, it contains letters I have received during the past year that relate to the contents of this book. Some of these letters were written by adults who wished to share some thoughts on giftedness with the book's young readers; other letters were written by gifted children themselves and are intended to be read by other gifted children; still more notes came directly to me from children and adults who just had something to say. Some letters began, "I'm too old to answer your survey . . ." or "I heard you wanted letters about being gifted . . ." and then went on to elaborate on particular impressions on the pros and cons of being smart.

Two of the chapter's letters were "commissioned" by me to Colin Camerer and Eric Grevstad. These two young men, now in their twenties, were contributors to the book *On Being Gifted,* a book written in the mid-1970s. *On Being Gifted* was written by two dozen gifted teenagers to help other bright adolescents deal with the fact of growing up gifted. In a sense, *On Being Gifted* is similar to this book, but written by older, more mature students. Colin and Eric are now able to reflect back on being gifted children, and they offer advice and wisdom to this book's younger group.

Gifted Children Writing to Other Gifted Children

Dear Friend,

I don't need to sacrifice talent to get along with others, but I can tell you (if that's the case with you), don't sacrifice your talent. You can just as easily, probably better, get along with other gifted children. If you do waste talent, think—you might have knowledge that would raise the knowledge of the whole world. That's a lot at stake!   GIRL, 11, MICHIGAN

Dear Friend,

I have been in a gifted program for about five months now, and I have felt the ups and downs. It's fun to learn about subjects that I never heard about before. We go on field trips and meet new friends. But it's not all easy. You have dittos and projects, and kids at school pick on you, so it is not all glamour.   BOY, 11, CONNECTICUT

Dear Friend,

Being in a gifted program is great. The kids are great and you feel like you've known them all your life. The teachers are the best and can help you with anything from acrophobia to zoos. I should know—I've been here since fourth grade and have never missed a day!

BOY, 11, CONNECTICUT

Dear Friend,

I heard that you just started going to a gifted program. Yayy!! There are some really good parts of these programs, like doing harder work and being around other gifted people. But one bad thing is that some of your old friends may tease you. Hang in there, though! That's how you can tell who your *real* friends are. If someone likcd you because you helped them with homework, then they'll be mad and tease you, and then you'll know they weren't *real* friends. But the ones who liked you because you were *you*—not because of your educational ability—are your real friends, and you'll know it.   BOY, 12, VIRGINIA

Dear Friend,

More than half of the kids in my gifted class have something to do after school. Maybe choir, band, clarinet, drama, swimming, tennis, soccer, or much more. (I've been in all of the above.)

If you are in all of those you are *bound* to get more friends, and the more popular you are, the more self-confidence you'll have. The more self-confidence you have, the more friends you'll make. It goes on and on.

GIRL, 12, CONNECTICUT

Dear Friend,

I lived in Pittsburgh, Pennsylvania, and wcnt to a small school. I was always ahead. I didn't even have to try to get straight *A*'s. But when I moved to Tulsa, I took a test to get into a gifted program and passed. Now, in my gifted program, I'm not the smartest kid anymore. There are other kids who are a lot smarter. This was hard for me at first, but now I'm used to it. This gifted program gives me a challenge.   GIRL, 12, OKLAHOMA

Dear Friend,

Being gifted means you have the *ability* to learn more than average children, but the gift does you no good if not used to its full potential. I think it is sad when someone doesn't use this gift, for God would not have given someone this gift if he had not meant for them to do great things. The gift of being able to be intelligent is not something to sneer at, or to waste, or to overlook. Not enough people have this ability to just toss it over their shoulders. If you are gifted, don't pay attention to what children say about it— just remember, if you work to the best of your ability, and *you* know *your-*

self that you are doing what's right (which I must remind myself of often when I'm under peer pressure), that's all that counts.

GIRL, 13, GEORGIA

Dear Kids,

If your peers make you miserable, ignore them and be proud of your special ability. Teasing (in this case) is most likely a synonym for jealousy. If you're teased, don't give in and lose your talent. Think of the good things—catching on quick to games, activities, whatever, and special opportunities others might not get.

If you're ever the only one who answers questions for a teacher, and after a few questions you become aware that your classmates are talking about you, don't stop answering to suit your peers. They probably won't be satisfied anyway. Besides, if you do, the teacher certainly isn't going to think you're smart. Now that's a total waste.

Do you hate being at the head of your class, and do you think your peers hate it too? Take a word or two of advice: don't put yourself down. The self-hate is usually stronger. Rejections and resentment from your peers may create unnecessary pressure for you. I've heard "don't attempt the impossible." So, what's impossible?

Man flying? We do.

Man walking on the moon? We do.

Man flying without a machine?

Miracles happen, brilliant inventors are born, so why can't man fly without machines? Someone *could* invent a way to fly like a bird. So . . . what's impossible? From my point of view, nothing . . . absolutely nothing!

GIRL, 13, MICHIGAN

Gifted Children Writing To Me

Dear Jim,

Even if my answers aren't put in your book, I'm glad you gave us kids a chance to tell what *we* feel.

GIRL, 11, ILLINOIS

Dear Jim,

When I first became involved with the gifted program in school, I was nervous and afraid that my friends would laugh at me. I was afraid that they would think I was "too good for them" and I'd not be accepted into the crowd.

I became ashamed of being gifted and at times I felt guilty, as if I had done something wrong. This period of time might have been very frustrating and depressing if it weren't for my gifted teacher.

She helped me to realize that being gifted is special, and you should be proud, not ashamed of it. Oh yes, I was still put down, but that didn't matter as long as I had my gifted classes. My whole life centered around them. They were my special place where I could express my opinions and not be laughed at. They were my place of freedom.

GIRL, 11, CONNECTICUT

Dear Jim,

In our gifted class we have many times talked about how it's maybe unfair that sports stars are popular and proudly wear their team coat. What about letter sweaters or pins for exceptionally high students? Are they as popular as stars in sports? Most likely not. Why?

GIRL, 11, MICHIGAN

Dear Jim,

These are my feelings on being gifted:

A Afraid that at some point in time I'll slip and do something wrong and everyone will notice.

G Guilty, when pressured into not doing my best.
I Isolated, when others make me feel left out of "the group."
F Frustrated, when I do something great and everyone laughs.
T Terrified, when I don't know the answer and everyone stares at me.
E Excited, when I create something that everyone appreciates.
D Disgusted, that my special needs are neglected.

P Privileged, when I get extra time during school to do something for myself.
E Embarrassed, when the teacher announces my grades.
R Relieved, when people don't laugh at me for getting less than 100%.

S Satisfied, when I am able to help someone else with something they
   don't understand.
O On top of the world, when somebody says they enjoyed my work.
N Nervous, when pressured to always be the best.

GIRL, 12, PENNSYLVANIA

Dear Jim,
   I live in a small town. We have a community college and a university.
Through the gifted program, twice a year I take mini-courses at the college
and university. These teachers give their time and knowledge and we all appreciate that.   BOY, 12, NORTH CAROLINA

Dear Jim,
   Some of my peers are rich and so are many families. My family is not
rich, but I feel I am richer than anybody I know. I am rich in knowledge.   GIRL, 12, ILLINOIS

. . . And One Letter From a Teacher

Dear Jim,
   Seven years ago, during my abbreviated experience as a student teacher,
I met a gifted nine-year-old whose name was John. His world was immense, his horizons boundless, and I never quite knew how to bridge the
gap between what he needed and what little I had to offer.
   When we met, it was in states of mutual innocence. Mine was an ideal-
ism about life and teaching. His was a precious wonderment—a fourth-
grader who was as comfortable with $E=MC^2$ as he was with balloons,
books, and baseball.
   Since that time, my exposure to students has made me fully aware that
we are not all equal, as much as we'd like to believe. The realm of environ-
ments and horizons, abilities and needs, is far too immense—and often
uncompromising. Repetitious daily routines for gifted children like John
are too empty, never really scratching below the surface where they long to
delve. Somewhere in this limbo, I exist and work—searching for solutions,
reaching to touch, attempting to make a difference.

Since 1978 my primary focus has centered on gifted students. To John, with his cherubic face, patiently explaining the mysteries of the Bermuda Triangle, I owe a world of thanks. He is one of the main reasons that I have immersed myself in the field of gifted child education. Now, understanding that I left too many voids for John and for other gifted students, I have started to bridge gaps.

One nine-year-old boy did all of this for me: he opened up my world, expanded my horizons, and gave me the courage to face the challenges that gifted programs can offer. To John (through you) I send my thanks—for a beginning—and thanks on behalf of all those students who are benefiting from my own growth.

Here's hoping you are still sliding down rainbows and chasing dancing stars, John—wherever you may be! DEBBY

Two Authors From *On Being Gifted* Write Again

Dear Kids,

I always disliked the word "gifted." A gift is something one is given, and presumably one then *owes* a gift in return. Somehow, the word makes smart people seem obligated to use their giftedness.

This is nonsense. The only thing people can rightfully demand from you is excellence—or at least an honest effort—in whatever you decide to do, whether it is ballet, engineering, economics, or rock music. In fact, the only reason you owe excellence in exchange for your gift is that you owe it to *yourself.* Don't be like the bright sixteen-year-old I met recently who wanted to major in two subjects—engineering and business—both red-hot fields brimming with job opportunities—so he could be assured of getting a comfortable job. When you have the ability to change the way the world spins, why worry about getting a job? You shouldn't.

"Genius" is another word I dislike. True genius requires creativity along with (or perhaps in spite of) intelligence. Studying, reading, and absorbing ideas invented by others require one impressive skill, but it is relatively easy to do. Much tougher is the invention of new ideas, and this can be painful, lonely, and difficult. Ph.D. programs at every university are littered with struggling, brilliant students who understand everything the teacher said, and nothing more—they learn, but cannot invent. Creativity and originality are not just *important* qualities, they are the *most* important qualities. It is important for bright kids at every age to be allowed and encouraged to think creatively, and to invent. Remember that "That's impossible" and "That's too wild an idea" are the favorite chants of the narrow minded.

Good luck (and stay hungry),

COLIN CAMERER, 24, ILLINOIS

Kids,

First, I want to say I've been very lucky. Not lucky to be gifted or to have been born smart or anything like that; in fact, I still get angry when people talk about me that way. I've been lucky because good things happened to me, and because my family and many teachers helped a great deal.

Another lucky break: I wasn't alone. Starting in first grade, there was a whole group of bright kids in my class, good at a lot of different things— spelling, math, playing ball. And grade school is a good time to do different things: in high school, some kids work on the newspaper and some are on the math team, and by the time you get to college, a football player can spend four years without meeting a theater major. Generally, the more organized things are, the harder it is to do more than one of them.

Which I suppose is the most important thing I have to say: people are going to try to organize you. Most people see others in terms of categories—friend, enemy, athlete, egghead—and being gifted, more than anything else, means that you decide not to fit into anyone's pigeonhole. That's not easy.

It's not easy for other people to deal with *you*, either. Especially with "back to basics," they'll be tempted to lump you in with everyone else. I had a grouchy, tired, near-retirement-age fifth-grade teacher; he not only didn't spend extra time with bright kids, he made me and another student do his lesson plans for the others. (There are a few teachers or people in authority who just don't like kids, gifted or otherwise; these people are deadly.)

On the other hand, don't let society put a "gifted" label on you to the extent of shutting you out of everyday things. The only thing worse than being denied opportunities is being forced to take them. In fourth grade, a teacher tried to make me read only Newbery Award-winning books, taking only the best from the library instead of *Encyclopedia Brown* and race-car stories. He meant well, in that I *was* a good reader and that kids *should* read Newbery books (some of them are fantastic); but some of them are pretty boring, and there are a lot of other books that are in between prize-winners and mindwasting trash.

I'm making this sound like a tightrope walk between being "gifted" and being "normal." That's exactly how it is; that's exactly how it's going to be for much of your life. You can't deny your talents; you shouldn't waste yourself by loafing at half or two-thirds of your capacity. (My folks taught me to read at two, but I went through part of first grade pretending I was no better than the beginners, going slowly and stopping a lot during reading-aloud sessions.) But you can't put yourself on a pedestal, or ignore the people you share the world with. They're worth knowing.

I haven't mentioned getting along with other kids. I don't have any sage advice about that, except that it's very important—more so than the stuff you learn from books or the chalkboard. It'll affect your academic decisions, too: I could have skipped sixth grade, for example, but my parents and I decided I wouldn't. For one thing, sixth grade was the big social year, with the week at camp and the end-of-school dinner; also, I was already up to a year younger than most of my classmates (my birthday's in September). I didn't particularly want to jump ahead to junior high. I wanted to avoid the image or reputation of not fitting in.

That's the problem. Some people don't look at you and see "better," they look at you and see "different." To minimize that, you have to work at it; you have to be friendly, be diplomatic, be honest without hurting people's feelings. It's better, when someone asks if you're smart, to say "in some things," which isn't lying. There's at least one thing that the person asking knows more about, or is better at, than you.

I'm 23 and I still think too much, take things too seriously, and envy people who I imagine don't even care that I do. It took me some time to learn that other people weren't having fun to spite me just as I wasn't being smart to spite them. (For a hot-shot gifted kid, I made a lot of mistakes and misunderstandings). The truth is, you're not the only one who's smart, and there's nothing that says you can't have fun. In fact, you can have more than most people.

Good luck,

ERIC GREVSTAD, 23, CONNECTICUT

PART II

Discussion Guide

This second section is designed to provide clues for discussing the concepts and practicalities of giftedness with children.

There is no "best way" to use them. Although each activity corresponds to a specific set of responses in Part I, it is likely that many of them could be equally as effective whether used before or after a reading of the children's comments. Similarly, readers may find many of activities stimulating to adult audiences—with parent groups or at teacher in-service workshops.

With Chapter One—Defining Giftedness

QUESTION A: WHAT DO YOU THINK BEING GIFTED MEANS?

1. Ask your students to select the one entry in this section that best expresses their *own* opinions about what giftedness is. To this selection, have them provide a brief rationale as to why this comment is, for them, better than the others.

2. Using the entry just selected, compare each child's definition or impression of giftedness with the definition of giftedness used in the school they attend. How well do the two mesh? Which definition is preferred by each child? Examine the reasons for individual children's preferred definition.

QUESTION B: ARE YOU GIFTED?

1. Select several responses where students have said they were gifted for other-than-academic reasons (e.g. motivation, creativity, heredity). Discuss the role of these other factors in relation to each student's personal definition of giftedness.

2. Have each student list at least two persons who would probably classify him/her as gifted. Then, have each student state *why* this person would have this impression. Next, tell each student to give the name of at least one person who does not think s/he is gifted. Again, have each student

provide a reason for this person's impression. From this information, a discussion about the nature of giftedness can begin.

QUESTION C: HOW DID YOU FIND OUT THAT YOU WERE GIFTED?

1. What came first . . . the suspicion or the label? Have each student review this section to determine how many of the respondents *thought* they were gifted before anyone told them so. Then, poll each of your own students on this same question of how each determined whether s/he was gifted.

2. Ask each of your students to explain how and when s/he discovered s/he was gifted. Using the comments made by children in response to "How did you find out you were gifted?", ask your students to examine whether their giftedness was discovered by themselves (due to early reading or "when school was easy," etc.) or whether someone else determined their giftedness for them (for example, a teacher, an IQ test score, a parent). If anyone at home or school helped individuals define or better understand what the term "gifted" meant, have them review the explanations they received. For those who never had the meaning of "giftedness" explained to them, ask them to recall their initial impressions of and reactions to the term. Lastly, ask each of your students to give one or several reasons why s/he is gifted, that is, "What talents or abilities of yours are so strong that people notice them?"

QUESTION D: HOW ARE YOU THE SAME AS AND DIFFERENT FROM OTHER CHILDREN YOUR AGE?

1. Review the comments in this section and invite your students to notice what these children consider the positive differences and the negative

differences of being gifted. Have your students devise similar lists of positive and negative differences.

2. Group students into pairs and have them discover ways in which they are the same as and different from their partners. Begin with the obvious (i.e. sex, hair color) but then, through brief interviews, have the students look for less-apparent characteristics. End by discussing the fact that even though gifted children share many similarities, their individual likes, dislikes, and strengths make them a diverse group.

QUESTION E: WHAT IS YOUR OPINION ABOUT BEING GIFTED? WHAT IS YOUR REACTION TO THE TERM "GIFTED"?

1. Ask each child to locate the one entry in this section that best sums up his or her personal reaction to the term "gifted." Instruct each student to add one or two sentences to this statement that personalizes the thought they have just chosen.

2. Many of the children's responses in this section refer to the negative connotations of the term "gifted"; however, few children suggest alternatives to this word. After having read this section, have your students decide if "gifted" is the best term to describe persons of high abilities. Have dissenting students select a term they believe is more appropriate and have them explain why their term is better.

QUESTION F: SOME SCHOOLS HAVE SPECIAL PROGRAMS AND TEACHERS FOR GIFTED STUDENTS. IS THIS A GOOD IDEA?

1. Review the preceding comments, then list the pros and cons for gifted programs as recorded by the respondents. Follow up on this by asking your students to add their own opinions to either or both lists. Then, using these two sets of comments as their bases of judgment, ask them

to vote on the appropriateness of offering special programs and teachers for gifted students.

2. As a class, devise a set of criteria by which students would permit other students to enter a gifted program. The children may wish to consider such factors as IQ, school grades, classroom behavior, teacher ratings, or self-nominations.

   Once the class has arrived at a system for identifying gifted children, compare it with your school's own criteria. Discuss the flaws and merits of the two systems.

QUESTION G: FOR THOSE OF YOU IN GIFTED PROGRAMS, WRITE DOWN HOW YOU FEEL ABOUT THIS PROGRAM.

1. Use the criteria developed by the children for inclusion in their gifted program (Question F, 2 above) as a basis for determining what skills and attitudes a student *in* their gifted program could expect to acquire. Compare these expected skills and attitudes with those currently fostered in your pupils' own gifted program.

2. Reread with students some of the specific reasons cited for liking gifted programs. Divide the responses into two areas, "academic advantages" and "other advantages," and discuss these items in relation to your own gifted program. Do the same activity, then, citing the "disadvantages," academic and otherwise, of gifted program participation.

ACTIVITIES FOR FURTHER DISCUSSION

Gifted children, while being able to conceptualize that intellectual differences exist among persons, nevertheless may question their own academic and social abilities. Also, some bright children wrestle internally with the concern of whether possessing superior talents places them in unwanted roles as "outsiders" or "weirdos." Open discussion of their specific concerns will increase awareness of ways that gifted children are both similar to and different from their agemates. For example:

1. Have each student select the one entry from each of the previous six sections that best represents his or her reactions to the issues raised. Compile this composite of responses and have each student write or state a brief, personal summary on being gifted.

2. Have each student list four things s/he can do very well—academic, athletic, and social skills are all good starters. Next, have the children write a similar list of skills they would like to improve. Then, using these lists, have each student walk around the room trying to find a classmate who:
   a. wishes to learn something s/he does well
   b. could teach him/her a skill s/he'd like to improve
   Follow up on this search by allowing the teaching/learning between pairs or small groups of students to take place.

3. Ask children—alone or in groups—how they react to the term "gifted" when it is applied to them. Have them read the following responses from children, then ask each child to align him or herself with the answer that is most representative of their own reaction to being labeled "gifted."
   a. "It's really neat to be special, not just another person, but somebody who has a great talent and is recognized for it."
   b. "Being called gifted isn't really fun, but it's not all that bad either. Sometimes people on the street will point at me and say, 'Hey, that's the kid from that smart class.' I don't like this but I've learned to take it as it comes."
   c. "I don't like being called gifted because other kids get jealous and angry at me."
   Be ready to hear that it's difficult to agree with one of these impressions more than another, for each seems right at different times. Use *this* reaction as a discussion-starter on the mixed reactions that many persons share about the label "gifted."

4. Read the following poem, written by a twelve-year-old girl, to your students. Ask for written responses—a letter, a story, another poem—that might serve to reassure the author that she is not alone.

ASKING A QUESTION

Proudness settles inside me
while shame begins to
surround me.
Trying to ignore those turning heads,
Trying to block out those cruel whispers
As my hand creeps slowly
higher.
I'm never really accepted.
I'm so different.

With Chapter Two—Getting Along With Friends and Classmates

QUESTION A: HOW DO FRIENDS REACT TO YOUR ABILITIES? WHAT DO THEY DO OR SAY THAT MAKES YOU FEEL GOOD OR BAD ABOUT BEING GIFTED?

1. Many children report that those friends who treat them the best are those who are likewise gifted. Perhaps this is to be expected, but it raises the question of how the term "peer group" relates to gifted children.
   Ask each pupil to write down, in private, the names of his or her best friend(s). For each friend named, have your students give specific reasons *why* this person is so special. Next, have each child examine his or her own list, noting if the children named:
   a. are also considered gifted
   b. are older, younger, or the same age as they.
   Review, then, the fact that "agemates" are not necessarily "peers," and that persons often get along best with those others who share both their abilities and interests. To highlight these points further, bring in your own high school yearbook and review which of your classmates were and were not your "peers"; then, have your students question you as to the reasons behind your selection of high school friends.

2. When someone gives you a sincere compliment—a smile, some genuine praise, a pat on the back—this compliment is called a "warm fuzzy." When someone makes fun of you, puts you down in front of others, or sticks out his tongue at your 100% spelling grade, we call *that* a "cold prickly."
   Review with your students the various "warm fuzzies" and "cold pricklies" that children refer to in this section of responses. Make a

chart of both, and invite students to elaborate on any particular comment that they, too, have heard or given. Next, add a column for "possible comebacks" to these "fuzzies" and "pricklies." "Thank you" or "It's nice to know you like my work" are good responses to compliments, while "It makes me feel bad when you call me a brain" might be an appropriate follow-up to a particular "cold prickly." Ask your students to come up with their own warm and cold comments and comebacks. Then, post your pupil-devised chart on a bulletin board and refer to it each time a kind or harsh word is passed between your pupils.

QUESTION B: ARE THERE EVER TIMES WHEN YOU TRY TO "HIDE" THE FACT THAT YOU ARE GIFTED?

1. Ask your students to recall one specific incident in which they either hid an academic ability or felt like doing so. Then, for students who recall such an incident, have them discuss whether they chose to hide their abilities:

   a. due to their own embarrassment at being gifted,

   b. because they thought their friends would be more comfortable.

   Discuss, then, what reaction could occur as a result of assuming this false front.

2. Many of the responses in this section reveal a sense of aloneness on the part of the writer—that the writer, perhaps, is the only person in the world who tries to hide from others his or her academic abilities. Use these comments as a base for discussion with your pupils to discover if, indeed, each young writer *is* a *minority of one,* or the reverse, that the desire to hide one's abilities in order to more easily fit in is common among those who appear different from others. Continue with a discussion of whether a person who disguises abilities is "bad," and conclude with a review of alternative ways to respond to friends who make being gifted more difficult than necessary.

3. Several responses in this section reveal that some children have no problem at all admitting they are smart—"if you've got it, why not use it?" Ask your students to reread these responses and then arrive at possible reasons why it might be easier for *some* kids to be gifted than it is for others. Discuss whether "coming to grips" with giftedness (as noted in the last response above) is a goal towards which all gifted children should strive.

QUESTION C: IS THERE ANYTHING YOU WOULD LIKE TO SHARE ABOUT YOUR OWN REACTIONS TO BEING SMARTER THAN SOME OF YOUR FRIENDS?

1. The responses in this section show that people may think gifted children are bragging, when they are not, or that they are trying to "show off" when actually, the children are merely working at their own levels.

   If any of your students has experienced this dilemma, ask for volunteers to relate a specific incident to other class members. Perhaps one student was "put down" by classmates for always answering a teacher's questions; another student might have been embarrassed to share report card grades with other classmates for fear that people would make fun of "all *A*'s"; or a student may have had to lower his or her vocabulary level when speaking with children outside of the gifted program.

   Once the incidents have been presented to the class, ask for comments from other students. If another boy or girl has experienced a similar situation to the problem being reviewed, discuss how s/he dealt with the dilemma.

   Through this sharing, children may be able to pick up cues from their intellectual peers regarding strategies to use when others criticize them for merely using the talents they possess.

2. Ask your students to recall a specific incident with a friend that made them feel especially proud of their talents. Have them describe both the event that took place and the reasons that made it so memorable.

   Next, describe a time when each of your pupils thought s/he made someone *else* feel good about an accomplishment. How did each student know that the other person appreciated their comments? Finally, find similarities between these two memorable occasions.

ACTIVITIES FOR FURTHER DISCUSSION

1. Share Figure 1 with gifted children, blocking out the final two captions. Ask each child to complete an alternative response, then share each child's caption in a group setting. In my own work, using this cartoon as a stimulus, all ages of children and adults cluster around these few responses:
   "I cheated." (about 50% say this)
   "I guessed." or "I got lucky." (add another 25% or so here)
   "I *still* say I studied." (about 15%)
   "Never mind" or "Shut up, it's none of your business" or "I never get all *A*'s—sometimes I get *B*'s on purpose." (the remaining few responses)
   Examine how your set of responses compares with my own, and then discuss what each one means. For starters, ask these questions:
   a. "Why might someone (or, Why might you . . .) respond that you cheated when you know that's not true?"
   b. "Has anyone ever felt like Joey, and either said or wanted to say 'I cheated'? Why? If you *have* lied about getting *A*'s, how did this make you feel? How did others (friends especially) react to your saying you cheated or got lucky?"
   c. "How is the response, 'I cheated' similar to the response 'I got lucky'?"
   Then, you might discuss individuals' responses to the cartoon in light of this quote from a gifted teenager:

   > *Though I realized learning was a thrill, I suppressed the yearning or transformed it, in some cases even degraded it, in order to be accepted by peers. Consequently, frivolities won over.* [1]

---

[1] *On Being Gifted*, American Association for Gifted Children, New York: Walker and Company, 1978, pp. 14–15.

FIGURE 1: Feiffer's Fables

In the school I used to go to I got A's in all my tests.

And all the kids would ask me, 'How did you do it, Joey?'

And I told them, 'I studied.'

So they wouldn't play with me anymore. 'The brain' they called me, 'The professor.'

Even my father! 'I want you to be a normal American boy,' he yelled at me.

So we moved away in disgrace.

Now in the new school I go to I still get A's in all my tests.

And all the kids still ask me 'How did you do it, Joey?'

But now I tell them 'I cheated.'

It's great to be thought of as regular.

Conclude this activity with a discussion of other responses that are available to bright children who are questioned on their ability to get A's. Include both humorous and "put-down" responses, if raised by the children.

What might be the consequences of other, more honest responses? Invite children to attempt these new suggestions in future dealings with others who ask, "How'd ya do it?"

2. Invite your students to write a classified ad that begins with the words:
   "WANTED: One friend. Must be . . ."
   and have your students complete the ad with whatever qualities or char-

acteristics the person they are looking for must possess. Also, have each ad writer include those personal assets s/he could bring to benefit this imaginary friendship. You may make this activity more realistic by having children respond to that classmate's ad which best exemplifies what s/he is looking for in a friend and a friendship. (For less bias, keep all ads and responses anonymous—at least initially.)

3. Gifted children sometimes feel that high abilities set them apart from some of their agemates; that they do not "fit in" to a particular social group or clique. To help your students realize that gifted children are similar to their agemates in many ways, use the following activity:
   a. cut out pictures from magazines of places people can go to be entertained—amusement parks, beaches, movies, museums, libraries, sporting events, concerts (rock or classical)
   b. post these photographs and have students put a check mark under their "Top Three" places to visit. Ask that each student keep a record of his or her choices
   c. repeat these first two activities with another class with the cooperation of a classroom teacher
   d. after these two classes of students have been surveyed, graph those places that seemed most popular for the combined class members (perhaps a few members from each class can help in compiling the data)
   e. have each student from both classes compare his or her own personal preferences with that of the group.

   This activity can help gifted students (and others) realize that many of their interests are shared by children outside of their class. Similar surveys can be conducted on such topics as "favorite foods," "favorite movies," "the best qualities in a friend," or other "bests" that your students can devise. The end purpose of each survey is the same: to establish a common base of similarities between gifted children and their agemates.

4. Consider ways in which schools and teachers intentionally group children by ability. Begin with reading groups (usually termed the "Bluebirds," "Robins," etc.), and move on to special education programs, bands or choruses, and (in junior high) classes limited to students with

particular abilities, such as foreign language or pre-algebra. Discuss the benefits and flaws of this system in terms of both educational reasons and peer relations. Suggest changes that could be made that might make each educational program more accessible to or understandable for non-participants.

With Chapter Three—Expectations:
Yours and Others'

QUESTION A: WHAT DO YOU EXPECT FROM "A PERSON
WITH YOUR ABILITIES"?

1. Gifted children often see themselves in terms of the strengths they *don't*
have rather than those they do possess. Sometimes bright children look
at other classmates with envy, as they assume that "everyone but me"
is good at sports or socializing.

In an activity designed to bring children in touch with their own individual strengths, you should ask each of your students to create a com-
mercial or advertisement about himself. Using words, pictures, photographs, speeches, or slogans, each pupil should take the time to "sell"
himself/herself, based on personal strengths. The task for each child is
to represent himself/herself in a series of positive images that convinces
both self and others that "I am worthwhile!" Share each student's com-
mercial with other class members in an effort to show to *all* class members the unique strengths of individual students.

2. Many bright children feel that the grades they get in school in no way reflect
their intellectual abilities—some resent the fact that they can get *A*'s without
trying, while others bemoan teachers who grade "gifted" students on a
harder scale than students not identified as gifted. In this regard, discuss
with your students "What makes an *A* worth getting?" Have each pupil review whether a high grade in a hard subject is more meaningful than an
equivalent mark in an easy subject. Devise a checklist, then, under the title
"How To Know When an *A* Means Something" to help students synchro-
nize their achievement with their expectations. Next, have your students
discuss ways to measure pupil progress and achievement by other than re-

port card grades. Ask them to consider peer- and self-evaluations, and devise some specific forms these evaluations might take.

QUESTION B: WHAT DO OTHERS—ADULTS OR FRIENDS—EXPECT FROM YOU, "A GIFTED CHILD"?

1. The following activity is useful in discovering your students' self-expectations and also those expectations they perceive that others have for them. Ask each of your students to complete the "sentence stems" below:
   a. When I get an A in school . . .
   b. Most of my friends expect me . . .
   c. When report cards come out . . .
   d. I do best in school when . . .
   e. I like school when . . .
   f. I like my friends best when . . .
   g. Some of my teachers . . .
   h. If I fail a test . . .
   i. When I get a compliment about my work . . .
   j. No one expects me to . . .
   Once the activity is completed, ask your students to swap lists with classmates and compare the lists. Allow time for sharing and discussion among these teams, and then ask for volunteers to comment on any responses that were particularly surprising or revealing.
   As a follow-up activity, create your own sentence stems, using parents or any other persons as the focus of the responses.

QUESTION C: HOW DO OTHERS REACT WHEN YOU MAKE A MISTAKE? HOW DO YOU REACT WHEN YOU MAKE A MISTAKE?

1. Although few persons actually expect gifted children to always be good or to always do well, bright children may believe that they are not sup-

posed to make mistakes. One of the best ways to prove to your students that, indeed, everyone *does* make mistakes is to admit openly to them some of your own. For example,
  —if you are poorly coordinated
  —if you have a bad temper
  —if you sometimes burn a meal or bounce a check
  —if you sometimes take credit for something that you did not do
Admit these flaws to your students. By talking openly about your own errors of judgment or logic, you are helping to make mistakes "OK."

2. There are a number of clichés that address the idea that "we all learn through our mistakes." Ask your students to recall an incident in their own lives that proves this statement true. (As in the activity above, you may have to open the discussion by revealing an example from your own life.) Make a chart, labeling it "OOPS!", and list those errors that you and your students believe have taught a lesson or, in the long run, a new skill.

QUESTION D: DO YOU EVER DO ANYTHING "JUST TO GO ALONG WITH THE CROWD"? WHY OR WHY NOT?

1. There are a number of reasons for going along with the crowd—peer acceptance, to have someone to play with, to make it obvious that you are willing to do things other people like to do. Also, though, there are times and situations when you must say "no," and decide to act as an individual. Ask your students to review the comments in this section, looking for those instances where "going along" was considered too high a price to pay in order to be like everyone else. Then, ask each student to give an example of a real or hypothetical situation in which s/he *would* conform to group standards and another example of an occasion when s/he would *not* conform. Try, then, to distinguish when and why it is "OK" to go along at *some* times, while at others it is not acceptable.

2. Review the cartoon of the elves making shoes (Figure 2), one frame at a time. As your pupils read each section, ask what is happening. Discuss how a difference (Frame 1) becomes "weird" (Frame 2) only after peer pressure sets in. Ask each child to complete Frame 4 before you show it, and review the meaning of each possible response. For example, the response shown has *definitely* different implications than one where all the elves go "Tap-Tap-Tippy-Tippy". Talk of examples in *your* life where you either "Tap-tapped" or "Tippy-tippied," and review the positive and negative consequences that followed.

ACTIVITIES FOR FURTHER DISCUSSION

During one of their chats, Charlie Brown and Linus discuss another of Charlie's too-frequent defeats. "There is no heavier burden," Linus says, "than a great potential." Charlie Brown agrees, for he recognizes wisdom when he hears it.

With gifted children for whom expectations are set—and set high—by self and others, the benefits of being bright can be coupled with the fear of being less-than-perfect. In their responses, gifted children have revealed their inner and external pressures to achieve. Some have spoken of failure in terms of $B+$'s or less, and others have noted that mistakes (or their possibilities) are to be avoided at all costs.

For gifted children, it is easy to disappoint others, for every one of their "peaks" may be just someone else's plateau. As the adults responsible for giving children encouragement, praise, and punishment, we must remember this, and, too, we must remember that "gifted" is not synonymous with "perfect."

To help review these topics, and to share the understanding with children, the activities below are recommended.

1. Make a list of what kinds of things people expect you to do without asking your permission. Also, make a parallel list of those expectations you have of others (friends, parents, teachers) around you. Do people have a right to expect anything from you? Do you have a right to expect anything from others? What qualifies someone else's expectation as "OK"?

Frame 1

Frame 2

Frame 3

Frame 4

2. As *Solo* (Pyramid Films, 1971) begins, a mountain climber struggles for handholds on a smooth wall of rock. Next, he challenges another peak, this one snow-covered, and nearly loses his balance. Finally, the climber scales what looks to be one final cliff, and he scans his view: More peaks, dozens of them, and some higher than today's mountain. *Solo* is a film about an individual's struggle to succeed, and about the attainment of a goal. Further, it serves as an allegory to life, for even though *Solo*'s climber has reached his goal for today, tomorrow's peaks still wait.

Use this film with primary age gifted children and they will respond to the beauty, the color, and the bravado of the film's one character. Use it with gifted children in grades four and above and you may discuss other, more introspective issues, for example:

"Did you ever feel that no matter what good you did there's always something higher? When? Why? Give an example."

"How do you feel when you reach a goal towards which you struggled? How long does this first emotion last? What's your *next* reaction after the newness of success wears off?"

"What emotions accompany achievement? Place them in a sequence as you explain one time in life when you attained a goal."

Show *Solo*. It is brief (16 minutes), colorful, and though the film has no words, it says so much. (*Solo* is available through many media centers or film distributors for a small rental fee.)

3. Bright children are sometimes said to avoid taking risks; the uncertainty of outcome or the fear of attaining less than perfection are often given as reasons. However, by providing children with quick proof that "the impossible" *can* be done, you may teach your students the value of risk taking. In this regard, ask your pupils to "name ten things that cannot be photographed." After compiling this list, assign three students an instant camera and the task of photographing three of the ten items just listed as "impossible" to catch on film. Soon your students may find that the things they said couldn't be done—photographing air, atoms, justice, love, time—can, indeed, be captured on film. This activity, along with being fun, can boost self-confidence in attempting the difficult.

Other "impossibilities":

a. Go outside and find 1,000,000 of something. Prove it.

b. Communicate with a non-living thing.
c. Make a change in or add something to your school that will be of benefit to every student and teacher.
d. Take a trip to a place that doesn't exist and provide proof that you have been there.

With these as starters, your students will soon be presenting other options that challenge both their minds and their ambitions.

With Chapter Four—Schools That Work

QUESTION A: DESCRIBE A "TYPICAL" AND A "PERFECT" SCHOOL DAY.

1. Review the comments in this section where students describe their perfect school day, and have your students then write their own ideas as to what makes a school day perfect. Remind your pupils to mention academic and social occurrences in their descriptions. Then, ask each student to rate, by percent, how well their typical school day "measures up" to their own desires and expectations for a perfect school day.

QUESTION B: WHAT ACTIVITIES OR METHODS DO TEACHERS USE THAT MAKE LEARNING WORTHWHILE?

1. All teachers—before they become teachers—must go to college and take courses on how children learn. These methods courses are supposed to give would-be teachers the skills to make teaching/learning fun and exciting. Invite your students to prepare a brief outline for a course entitled "Teaching Gifted Students." Using the comments from this section as a base, and adding personal insights and opinions, ask your students to highlight what *they* believe should be emphasized in such a course. Request specific activities, methods, or attitudes that they believe are essential in preparing teachers to work with smart students. Review these guidelines in relation to your *own* teacher training program.

2. A simple activity: Ask each of your students to review in writing "the best thing that ever happened to me in school" or "the most important lesson I ever learned in school." Some students may list awards they received or teams for which they were chosen. Others may be more introspective and mention "lessons of life," such as "learning to get along with others" or "learning that I won't always be the top student."

Then, ask the children to write a short paragraph on why this one event/lesson is so memorable. (Hint: As a teacher or parent, you should participate in this activity by sharing your *own* written response with the children.)

QUESTION C: WHAT SHOULD BE DONE IN A GIFTED PROGRAM THAT IS DIFFERENT FROM THE REST OF A SCHOOL'S CLASSES?

1. Ask your students to consider the following questions:
   a. "What one thing have you learned about in your gifted program that is the most memorable?"
   b. "What one thing have you learned to *do* in your gifted program that is the most memorable?"
   c. "What was the one subject you learned in your gifted program that was better than you thought it would be? What was the most boring?"
   d. "What subject(s)/topic(s) would you like to research that have thus far not been covered in your gifted program?"
   e. "What advice would you give a friend who was considering whether or not to enter your gifted program?"
   Answers to these questions might serve the twofold purpose of evaluating informally the success to date of your gifted program and suggesting alternative activities/topics for future use.

2. Have your students chart their daily activities as they now exist in your gifted program and rate each activity on a scale of "1" (blah!) to "5" (excellent). Then, have groups of students devise "the perfect schedule," one that includes only those activities in which groups of students

would like to participate. Next, evaluate each item on these two lists in terms of all of the following:

a. hard v. easy
b. fun v. not fun
c. important v. trivial
d. creative v. logical
e. challenging v. boring
f. academic v. social

Does a single pattern emerge for characteristics of the "blah" activities in relation to the "excellent" activities? Does this evaluation of each gifted program activity suggest the need for any changes in what is offered to your students? If so, discuss what changes can be made. Can "boring" or "trivial" or "social" activities still be educationally sound? Discuss.

QUESTION D: WHAT COULD TEACHERS DO TO MAKE SCHOOL A BETTER PLACE TO LEARN FOR SMART STUDENTS LIKE YOURSELF?

1. Just as the tastiest of cakes is little more than the creative mixture of eggs, flour, and spices, so is school a combination of common ingredients. Using this analogy, ask your students to create a recipe for one of the following:

"The Perfect Teacher" "The Perfect Classroom"

Remind your students that a recipe includes both the ingredient itself and the amount of the ingredient needed, and that too much of anything might spoil the recipe. Also, remind them that a pinch of bitter—lemon, salt, baking chocolate—sometimes is needed for balance. (You may want to exclude yourself and your classroom from this exercise.)

After the recipe's ingredients for the teacher or classroom are completed, ask each student to give instructions for blending together these elements. Do you "stir," "beat," "mix," or "allow to cool"? Does one ingredient serve as a base into which other items are sifted?

When these recipes are completed, post them and have your students award a "blue ribbon" to the tastiest classroom and teacher.

2. Sometimes, students remember what they *dislike* about school a lot more quickly and a lot more often than recalling the positive events that occur in classrooms or on the schoolyard. To give students a chance to look back upon those activities or lessons that are particularly meaningful, ask your students to maintain weekly journals, into which they respond to these questions:
   a. What is the most important lesson I learned this week?
   b. What is the most important thing I learned about myself this week?
   c. Who was the most influential person in my life this week? Why?
   Invite students to keep their journals for a month or more, re-reading their previous comments each time they answer for a new week. Also, keep this journal yourself to see if it helps *you* see the brightest spots of your week.

QUESTION E: WE'VE TALKED A LOT ABOUT GIFTED
CHILDREN, BUT WHAT MAKES A TEACHER
"A GIFTED TEACHER"?

1. Recall for your students your own "favorite teacher ever." Tell them about one distinct incident that you remember that makes you smile each time you think of this teacher, and then elaborate further, providing additional specifics. Then, have your students itemize the characteristics they pick up about this person that makes him or her so special to you. Agree or disagree, as needed, with your students' impressions.

   Next, ask each of your students to recall his or her own favorite teacher and discuss the intellectual, physical, social, or other characteristics that have set this teacher apart from the rest. End the discussion by reviewing these specific characteristics in relation to "The Perfect Teacher" recipe completed in the previous section.

   You may wish to exclude yourself from consideration as your pupils' "favorite teacher ever" to avoid comments meant to please you or make you feel wonderful. Also, for children too young to have experienced many different teachers, you may compile a list of characteristics that the children believe *would* make a teacher "special."

2. Pretend that a committee has just been established that is responsible for hiring a new teacher for your town's expanding gifted program. The local school board members have decided that they would like a student representative to help in selecting the person to fill this job. This student member will be able to ask all applicants three questions—and only three questions.

Ask your students to consider, as a class, what issues should be addressed through these questions. Begin by brainstorming all the possible questions that might be asked, and then focus on the three most often asked questions.

Follow this activity by summarizing with your students those personal and professional characteristics that they select as most important for a teacher of gifted students.

ACTIVITIES FOR FURTHER DISCUSSION

Students have already reviewed many of the strategies teachers use to enliven classroom lessons: more involvement, fewer restrictions, and less time spent on the obvious. Also, though, there are instructional materials available to help teachers add enjoyment and depth to their teaching. The selections below are my personal "Top Five" for teachers wishing to expand both creative teaching *and* learning. The items are in no particular order, nor do they favor one content area over another. However, all the materials share these features:

—they invite creative responses from the students and teachers who use them

—their various authors and publishers recommend a variety of alternative methods for using the materials

—they are adaptable for use with children in primary grades through junior high school

—they don't break an already-strained budget (even if you buy all five)

—I've used them all—again and again.

Reference #1: *The Brown Paper School Book Series,* published by Little, Brown and Company, 34 Beacon Street, Boston, Massachusetts 02106.

This series consists (at present) of eleven books, each about 125 pages and each reviewing a topic of interest to many children. The books' authors are "a group of California teachers, writers and artists who get together every now and then to work on stuff for kids and to have a good time. They believe learning only happens when it is wanted; that it can happen anywhere and doesn't require fancy tools."

Books in the *Brown Paper* series include:

The Book of Think—or How to Solve a Problem Twice Your Size
Excellent tactics are listed for tackling and overcoming nuisances and commonplace problems such as "how to cope with a friend who always tries to get you in trouble" or "getting out of touchy situations by using logic and creativity".

The 'I Hate Mathematics!' Book
This book shows how volume—and probability and logic and decibels—are *all* part of the world of math that surrounds us.

The Reasons for Seasons
The title says it all.

My Backyard History Book
Every backyard has a history, and this book explains methods of finding it.

Everybody's A Winner
Exercise and physical education are reviewed in this primer on fitness.

Blood and Guts
In this book, the would-be physician learns about anatomy and bodily functions through some real-life (but safe!) experiments on self and others.

I Am Not A Short Adult
A guide to being a kid in a world where "acting your age" somehow doesn't always work.

Other recent books in this expanding Series include *Beastly Neighbors: All About Things In The City; Make Mine Music; The Book of Where, or How To Be Naturally Geographic;* and *The Night Sky Book.*

Reference #2: *Thinklab I* and *II*, published by Science Research Associates (SRA), 155 N. Wacker Dr., Chicago, Illinois 60606

Each *Thinklab* is a cluster of 120 activity cards stressing logical and critical thinking. Each card is a mini-lesson, and a clever color-coded scheme lets users cross reference activities that involve the same thinking skills. A charting system keeps track of cards completed by each student (or teacher). *Thinklab* cards can fill a stray five or ten minutes of classtime in a most productive and thought-provoking manner.

Reference #3: *ESSENCE I* and *II*, published by Addison-Wesley, Reading, Massachusetts 01867

ESSENCE materials are not your typical science texts—they're better (and they're not texts). The designers of *ESSENCE* view the whole *world* as a science lab, and in their two sets of about 100 cards each, they present activities that invite exploration. For example:

"Go out in your community and find who are predators and who are prey. What happens when predator and prey change places? (P.S. Watch out for this one if you get into people—high community threat!)"

"Go outside and find evidence that something natural has taken place."

"Go outside and find joy in your environment."

Each card presents a full lesson, and in *ESSENCE II*, the activities are based on particular themes (*e.g.* astronomy, psychology, movement, "people patterns"). Also, *ESSENCE* materials blend together content and feeling, as students are urged to consider the effects of science on everyday life. Recommended for use in kindergarten through graduate school, the two kits invite adventure through thoughtful observation.

Reference #4: *Celebration of Creativity,* published by the Nebraska State Department of Education, 301 Centennial Mall South, Lincoln, Nebraska 68508

Probably the biggest bargain today for educators interested in creativity theory and training, this book provides a yearful of activities based both *in* content areas (math, reading, history, etc.) and *on* the past work of leading authorities in creativity. Each activity is teacher-designed and has been tested in a classroom, and the Teacher's Edition is a fine introductory course in creative thinking, teaching, and feeling.

Reference #5: *Jackdaws,* published by Viking Penguin Inc., 40 West 23 St., 10010

From the *Spanish American War* to *Women's Rights* to *Westward Ho!,*

Jackdaws kits explain history in terms of events precipitated by people—little people, usually, who, in turn, effect the decision-makers' choices. Actual documents—letters, newspapers of the day, memos, maps—are enclosed in each *Jackdaws* unit so that you can help your students to relive history piece by piece. Available for purchase separately or in a complete package, *Jackdaws* provides the basis for much discussion regarding the "who, where, and why" of historical events.

With Chapter Five—When Schools Fail

QUESTION A: DESCRIBE YOUR "TYPICAL" SCHOOL DAY.

1. Several students in this section relate "tales of woe" about too much homework. At the same time, though, these students refer to school as "more of the same" or ". . . review, review, review." The two comments seem contradictory, as homework would not be needed if the topic under study were familiar. Nonetheless, the situation as presented in these pupils' comments is probably an accurate representation of situations existing in many schools. If *yours* is one of these schools (get your students' opinions on this), ask your pupils to devise a remedy for this situation. Perhaps they will write a homework policy, or revise an existing one, that gives credit for knowledge already learned; or maybe they can develop a system or schedule that allows them time (to work on homework at school rather than at home.) In any event, if your students take the initiative to "fix" a presently uncomfortable situation regarding homework or classroom review, plan to implement the idea with at least one teacher, in at least one subject.

2. Much controversy in recent years has centered around the lack of basic skills that students have when they graduate from eighth grade or high school. In response to these criticisms, much attention has been paid to returning to the basics of the three Rs. However, many gifted children complain that *too much* time is spent on the basics, leaving little time for enrichment activities. Ask your students to comment on how they believe basic subject matter should be taught to students with high abilities. Ask for personal examples of how the existing curriculum was (or could have been) changed to take their advanced abilities into consideration.

QUESTION B: WHAT HAPPENS TO YOU IN SCHOOL THAT
MAKES LEARNING MORE DIFFICULT OR LESS INTERESTING?

1. If the reactions in this section have any basis in truth, then some gifted
   students believe that teachers can actually hinder their progress. Surely
   this is neither the teachers' goal nor intention—yet still, for some students, the perception is real.

   Discuss with your pupils the one teacher behavior that bothers them
   the most. Perhaps it will involve teacher expectations ("She thinks that
   just because I'm gifted, I understand everything!"), or maybe it will be
   a behavior ("Let's all review long division just one more time.") Review how and why a change in a teacher's behavior or attitude would
   make school more inviting.

   (Note: This activity is not meant to "single out" bad teachers and discuss their flaws. Tell your students that the purpose behind this activity
   is to effect positive change, not to judge particular teachers' skills.
   Also, as your pupils make suggestions for change, you might remind
   them of two realities:
   a. the usual class has 20 to 30 children besides him/herself
   b. suggestions, if stated in a positive tone, often have a greater effect
      than a powerful, but negative, "manifesto.")

2. Each student has a personal history, filled with both high points and hurdles that have left a permanent effect. Ask your pupils to "get in touch"
   with their own backgrounds by making a time-line that begins with
   "My birth" and ends with "Today." Between these endpoints, have
   the students leave plenty of room on the paper to fill in important events
   or occasions. Individual children may wish to concentrate on goals they
   attained ("making the swim team"; "getting on the honor roll") or
   happy or sad events ("my trip to Disney World"; "my aunt died") at
   both home and school. Once the children have placed some important
   events chronologically on the time-line, ask them to go back and review
   how many items listed relate to school. Discuss these events in terms of
   the influence that going to school has had on their life.

   Additionally, you may wish to have the students extend their personal
   time-lines into the future, plotting hopes, dreams, and goals they wish
   for themselves in the years ahead.

QUESTION C: DO YOU EVER GET BORED IN SCHOOL? IF "NO," WHY NOT, AND IF "YES," WHAT DO YOU DO TO RELIEVE THE BOREDOM?

1. Woody Allen once stated that, for him, "90% of life is just showing up." Interpret this quote for your students by reviewing those times, events, or situations in your *own* life when you just "showed up," put in your time, or tolerated boredom. Ask each student to review times in and out of school when s/he did the same. Next, discuss whether there are any benefits of boredom, and whether being bored can teach you anything—if so, what? End this discussion with another quote (this one anonymous): "The cure for boredom is curiosity; there is no cure for curiosity," and its relevance to your students' analyses of the benefits of being bored.

2. Take the letters of the word boring—B-O-R-I-N-G—and write one word that begins with each of the six letters and that represents something that can be done to *relieve* boredom. For example:
   B: Bake
   O: Open a bartering service
   R: Read
   I: Independent study project
   N: Notice something new
   G: Grow plants
   Then, post each student's list on a bulletin board, using this board as a ready reference for students who complain, "There's nothing to do—I'm bored."

ACTIVITIES FOR FURTHER DISCUSSION

In the children's classic *The Wind in the Willows*, the Water Rat floats down a river in a blue and white boat for two. He is talking to his shipmate about the simple joys to be had by exploring. There is "nothing," he says to Mole, "absolutely nothing half so much worth doing as simply messing about . . . simply messing."

The gifted children in this chapter and in the previous "Schools That Work" chapter refer to these same pleasures. They talk of teachers who allow them to experiment and explore their world; they mention hands-on activities as being as valuable a method of instruction as lecture or reading; they seek out the everyday adventures involved in asking questions that have no (or many) answers, or experimenting with the raw data of mud or clay or half-baked ideas: "Simply messing."

The activities and methods that follow are intended to provide teachers with alternative ways to approach classroom instruction. Some of the five suggestions are based in sound educational theory, while others are just new twists to common sense and logic. One feature the activities have in common is that they all *can* work to the benefit of your bright students.

TECHNIQUE #1: LEARNING BY DOING

At each grade level, students must master a series of academic requirements ("objectives") as proof that learning has occurred. The usual methods for providing this proof are tests or book reports or research papers. These formats are fine, but for gifted students to whom mastery of content comes quickly, school may become a sequence of consistently well-done but similar essays on "Why I Liked This Book" or "A 500 Word History of the Civil War." To break these patterns, you may suggest to your students ways to alter their *styles* of reporting; although the content and topic remain the same, the mode of presentation differs. For example, using the Civil War theme, your students might prove competency by designing:

a. *a newspaper advertisement* written to entice young men to become Union or Confederate soldiers. (Surely a well-written ad would include proof that some factual knowledge regarding the reasons for the Civil War has been learned.)

b. *a coloring book*—twenty pages or so—that illustrates important persons, places, and events of the Civil War (and can be used to teach younger children about this phase of American history.)

c. *a speech* for or against slavery or secession or conscription, as presented from the biases of a northerner or southerner of 1863.

The list of alternative methods to prove competency is endless. A few other learning-by-doing options include:

banners	mobiles
biographies	models
blueprints	mosaics
brochures	newspapers
cartoons	paintings
charts	pantomimes
crossword puzzles	plays
debates	poems
dioramas	posters
experiments	scrapbooks
games	sculptures
graphs	skits
interviews	songs
maps	tapes
masks	time-lines

Every classroom activity can be made either dull or exciting, depending upon your own level of imagination and input. But with just a little originality, lessons and assignments can be *both* educational and fun.

TECHNIQUE #2: THE IMPORTANCE OF "HOW TO" SKILLS

For gifted children who wish to explore topics and work on projects that are new or unfamiliar, they may find it hard to go very far without some basic "how to" skills. "How to" skills come in many varieties. Perhaps the most common how-to need for school children involves library research—how to use the card catalog or microfiche reader; how to go beyond the encyclopedia to locate facts and other information; how to take notes, read maps, or use indexes, almanacs, and computers.

Also, for children who plan to complete a project using one of the methods in "Technique #1," "how to" skills may involve the making of slides or the use of a camera. If interviews are to be done, then the student must learn how to question incisively; if blueprints are to be drawn, then a knowledge of "scale," "perspective," and the jargon of architects must come first; if songs are to be written or skits performed, a "how to" lesson on choreography or set design may be helpful. It is frustrating to begin a project with little more than a "good idea" as a base. Gifted children, despite their many obvious talents and capabilities, may still need instruction in the proper use of the "tools" of whatever "trade" they wish to explore. *Provide* these prerequisites or, if you are unable to do so, locate individual books, manuals, or persons that *can* provide the necessary "how to" assistance when students begin to explore new areas of interest.

TECHNIQUE #3: QUESTION QUALITY

Several children in this chapter complain about teachers whose methods of questioning involve little more than a quick repetition of facts. These same students applaud teachers who allow classroom discussions or who reinforce basic skills with activities that encourage creative thinking. One of the ways teachers can ensure that their bright pupils benefit most from in-class discussion and review is to consider their *own* question-asking skills. Do the questions asked require any more than one-word answers? Is there more than one correct answer to questions whose responses are based on opinion or judgment? Do your questions involve the interpretation of data rather than its mere recall? The question categories listed in the table show several ways teachers can quiz students on the extent of their knowledge about basic facts . . . and beyond.

QUESTION CLASSIFICATION CHART
CONTENT AREA: SOCIAL STUDIES

NARROW OR CLOSED QUESTIONS	TEACHER QUESTION	STUDENT RESPONSE MODE
1. Recall questions	Who was our country's first president?	Recall from memory; respond with a name, date or place; define a term; answer yes or no.
	What is "Manifest Destiny"?	
	Is the Indian Ocean larger than the Atlantic Ocean?	
2. Convergent questions	How are Seminole Indians like Sioux Indians?	Explain; compare and contrast; apply known information.
	Why don't citrus plants grow well in Iowa?	
	How does "supply-side economics" operate?	

BROAD OR OPEN QUESTIONS	TEACHER QUESTION	STUDENT RESPONSE MODE
1. Divergent questions	In what ways might our country be different today if the South had won the Civil War?	Make implications; give an opinion; hypothesize; predict outcomes.
	What would life be like in our town for the survivors of a nuclear war?	
	What do you believe would be a good amendment to the U.S. Constitution?	
2. Evaluative questions	Is it a good idea to develop nuclear power?	Defend an opinion; choose among alternatives; make a value judgment.
	Should society have the authority to determine who may have children?	
	Should handicapped children attend regular elementary schools?	

In no way is this chart intended to show the desirability of "open" over "closed" questions—indeed, there are times when one-word or short answers are preferred. Instead, it is meant to reinforce what we already know: that not all questions have answers (while some do); that questions can serve as a starting point from which to begin discussions (as well as being a way to end discussion of a topic already reviewed); and that learning occurs through asking and wondering (as well as telling and explaining).

Open questions demand the use of a thought process we do not quite understand but that we nonetheless consider "good"—some call this process *creativity*. Closed questions demand the ready recall of facts or observations that lead to a single conclusion. In educating gifted children, both forms are required.

Technique #4: Wait Time

Studies at Columbia University show that 70% of classroom talk is *teacher* talk—that one person, the instructor, is in charge of seven out of every ten minutes of classroom time. This proportion is neither inherently bad nor high—indeed, the purpose of education *is* to teach, and this is often done through direct instruction. However, a statistic that bears notice within this 70% is one that involves "wait time." Wait time is the span that exists between the moment a question is asked and the subsequent response *to* this question. If you are an average teacher (as regards wait time), this time lapse is approximately one second. In other words, in the small amount of time it takes a student to cough, clear a throat, or wink, you have probably already solicited a response to a question on rocks or current events or the Civil War.

The implications of this one-second wait are obvious—with so brief a time to think or consider options, students will respond with answers that are short (one word or a short phrase), that are vacant of proof (there seems to be no time to elaborate), or that are fairly obvious ("When the temperature gets cold, water will freeze."). Further, if this one-second wait time occurs in lesson after lesson, it is safe to predict that the students who raise their hands are those who knew the question's answer *before* the question was asked.

The alternative? Wait a minimum of five seconds between asking a question and soliciting a response from a specific student. The results, then, might be the same as those reported by researchers at Columbia: longer student responses, increased pupil confidence that the response given is appropriate, and more evidence supporting why the answer given *was* given. Wait time: a seldom used and little understood boon to the education of *all* children.

TECHNIQUE #5: REAPPRAISING PRAISE

The Harvard Business Review seems an unlikely resource for classroom teachers who wish to improve their skills. However, in Richard E. Farson's 1965 article "Praise Reappraised," he asserts that in the business world, "praise" is synonymous with "evaluation." In our work as teachers, a parallel system is in effect. For example, when we praise a student for "a job well done," we imply that more of the same is expected. Further, the mere fact that we give praise implies that we are in the position to know quality in a student's products or efforts—which is usually true, but not in all circumstances. In fact, the praise we distribute may have an opposite effect to that intended. "When rewards (praise) are high, children tend to stop experimenting sooner than when the number of rewards is relatively lower. There is some reason to suspect that when children work on a complex task, rewards given by the teacher may interfere with logical thought processes."*

The lessons to learn from these researchers' work are clear: understand that praise may actually inhibit a child from further exploration, learn that praise is considered a subtle form of evaluation, and remember that the highest form of evaluation is that which one gives to oneself.

For gifted children whose goals are set (and set high!) by self and others, the role of praise and its implications are important to recall.

* Mary Budd Rowe, "Science, Silence and Sanctions," *Science and Children,* April, 1969

With Chapter Six—Parents: A Helping Hand from Home

QUESTION A: DO YOU EVER CATCH YOUR PARENTS
BRAGGING ABOUT YOUR ABILITIES OR COMPARING YOU TO
YOUR BROTHERS OR SISTERS? HOW DO YOU FEEL
ABOUT THESE COMPLIMENTS OR COMPARISONS?

1. The consensus among respondents in this section favors receiving compliments from parents or teachers. There are some times, however, when compliments are better received than at others. Ask your students to first read the comments in the "Bragging or Complimenting" section, and next, to determine when (and from whom) praise is most appreciated. Then, have students list times and situations in which receiving compliments makes them feel proud or comfortable, and others when they feel embarrassed. Review ways to *respond* to compliments—both those praises that are appreciated and those that are not. Lastly, role-play situations in which students must tell a well-intentioned adult that his or her compliment is embarrassing to receive (and the opposite, when it is most appreciated).

2. Sibling rivalry—the competition between offspring—has existed as long as have families. In Genesis, Joseph was hated by his brothers for finding special favor with his father. Without sibling rivalry, there would have been little conflict in *Cinderella*. Review the reality of sibling rivalry with your students and ask them if they are ever compared to their siblings; request specific instances of these comparisons. Following this review, examine whether the children remember most those comparisons which put them "on top" or "below" the sibling with whom s/he is compared.

End this discussion of sibling rivalry by devising a list, as a class, of ways that parents can encourage their children *without* using comparisons with siblings. For instance, ask your students, ''What could your parents say or do to encourage you to do your best work?'' Post this list, or send copies home with a cover letter explaining the context in which the suggestions were developed.

QUESTION B: WHAT HAVE YOUR PARENTS SAID TO YOU ABOUT BEING GIFTED? WHAT EXPECTATIONS DO YOUR PARENTS HAVE OF YOU BECAUSE OF YOUR ABILITIES?

1. As a class, discuss ways in which your students' parents have helped them deal with and develop their high abilities. Pinpoint specific statements that parents have made, and review why these were helpful. Next, begin a discussion titled, ''Everything you always wanted to know about being gifted but which no one ever told you.'' During this time, review those things left unsaid by parents or other adults that would have been helpful to know or learn before they were discovered by the students.

2. Ask your students to write answers to these two questions:
   a. ''What would you *like* to be doing fifteen years from now?''
   b. ''What do you think your parents expect you to be doing fifteen years from now?''
   c. ''What do you *think* you will be doing fifteen years from now?''
   Compare each student's two responses and then, as a class, compare answers for similarities and differences. Next, ask students to exchange papers; it will then be the task of each student to integrate the responses to questions *a, b,* and *c* so that what each student would *like* to happen becomes a part of what they *think* will occur. Return the papers, then, to their owners, and have fun discussing the possibilities just suggested.

QUESTION C: WHAT HAVE YOUR PARENTS DONE TO GET
YOU INTERESTED IN NEW TOPICS, AND WHAT *HAVEN'T* THEY
DISCUSSED WITH YOU THAT YOU BELIEVE THEY SHOULD?

1. As a class, make a list of activities, topics, or situations that your students would not have been involved in were it not for a parent's influence. Next, list those activities, topics, or situations that students' parents have *forced* them into trying out, and another list of those ideas that were followed up by the children *despite* parental disapproval. Compare which of the above resulted in the most memorable times spent for the students. Highlight the positive benefits and negative consequences of parent involvement in their children's spare-time activities.

2. Conduct a poll of your students, asking the question that starts this section: "What haven't your parents discussed with you that you believe they should?" Do the same survey of other students in the school to determine if the topics that are generally avoided (e.g. sex, drugs, growing up) are also those that gifted students believe need discussing. Then, consult your school and town librarians, school guidance counselor, or social worker, to see if they are aware of books, films, or other methods that have proven themselves useful in convincing parents to discuss real-life issues with their children. Present any data that are accumulated to the school's PTO/PTA or similar group for their review and consideration.

QUESTION D: WHO OR WHAT MAKES YOU
HAPPIEST AT HOME?

1. It may sound morbid, but as an activity to invite introspection, it is very effective: ask each of your students to write his or her own epitaph. Remind them that most gravestone messages are short, sometimes comical, and always indicative of one or more important events in one's life. Post the gravestone slogans on a bulletin board, and have students guess who wants to be remembered for what. (This activity may pro-

duce a new interest in the epitaphs of historical or literary figures—a fine way to examine the past from a very different vantage point.) Keep the tone of this activity light, but be prepared to receive some interesting and insightful messages. And don't forget to do this activity yourself, too—this adds to its credibility and sense of purpose.

ACTIVITIES FOR DISCUSSION WITH PARENTS

The activities listed below are meant to be used by teachers in any discussions they may have with parents of gifted students. If used in a group setting, the activities may be helpful in defining several "do's and don'ts" about raising gifted children. Also, if my experience is any indication, the activities will spark discussion *among* parents, allowing each to reveal some of the high points and hurdles involved with raising bright children.

1. Gifted children sometimes feel that their parents expect them to perform well in all academic and social situations. In some cases, these views are reinforced by parents' actions more than their words. For example, one young teen has said: "They hindered me at times by often expecting too much of me. By being perfectionists, my parents made me feel inadequate and frustrated if I was not constantly performing at my best."*

   Share this quote and several others from the "Expectations" section of this chapter with parents of gifted children. Remind the parents to consider their influence as role models, and tell them that the best way to teach that perfection is not expected is to share some personal defeats, failures, or weaknesses with their children. "Make it real" by sharing some of your *own* unmet goals or underrealized expectations, continuing the discussion with a review of the fact that no one lives a life free of disappointments. End on a positive note—that despite your own lack of perfection, you continue to progress, grow, and enjoy.

* *On Being Gifted,* American Association for Gifted Children, Walker, 1978; p. 49.

2. A common mistake made by adults when giving praise is an error in focus—we praise the child instead of his or her act. For example, notice the difference in these two comments:

    "What a smart girl! Look at that report card!"

    "A report card with five *A*'s and two *B*'s! That shows real effort!"

   In the first instance, evaluation of the child's work as reflected in her grades is secondary in emphasis to bestowing flattery upon the child. While this seems like appropriate reinforcement, a child can come to associate her "smartness" and her "goodness" with her school performance. Consequently, if the next report card (or test, or footrace, etc.) falls short of this present effort, "I am bad" can be the self-judgment. The second statement primarily lauds the act, not its performer, which is the appropriate focus for a well-deserved tribute.

   Remind the parents of the power that praise can have—both negative and positive power—and practice with them some compliments that are directed appropriately, towards the child's *work*, rather than towards the child.

3. Just as parents of gifted children need to understand the power conveyed through giving a compliment, they also need to understand that they can defeat the *purpose* of their compliments if they couple their praises with the encouragement to do more. For example, the parent who says:

    "Four *A*'s and two *B*'s aren't bad, . . . BUT your work could improve."

    or,

    "You play the piano well, . . . BUT your little sister is catching up to you!"

    or,

    "Playing by yourself is OK, . . . BUT when I was *your* age I was a team player."

   is sending a "mixed review" to the child. The child, in turn, will most likely remember the message after the ". . . BUT," the encouragement to do more. Thus, despite a child's good or best efforts, s/he may begin to feel that "only perfection" is good enough to satisfy Mom or Dad.

   To remedy this dilemma, tell your students' parents to keep their two statements separate. Yes, Four *A*'s and two *B*'s *are* good. Period. The equally-as-valid assertion that "your work could improve" should be saved for another time, removed from the praise of a job well done. Once again, practice these skills with your pupils' parents. Talk of times in their own lives and work when compliments were coupled with an urge to do better, and ask *them* to recall which parts of the statements are still most vivid.

4. Many parents of gifted children might be surprised to read the comments expressed in this chapter. For example, it might be revealing to hear that bright children, for the most part, like compliments but abhor comparisons; that gifted children often feel overwhelmed by their parents' too-high expectations; that areas of discussion needing attention at home range from sex to school grades to banter about the day's mundane events.

Before reading some of the children's comments in this chapter, ask the parents the "adult versions" of the questions asked of the children. Ask them:

a. Do you, as parents, ever find yourselves bragging about or comparing your children? How do you think your children react to these comments?

b. What have you said to your child about being bright? Did your expectations change when your child was identified as gifted?

c. What do you do to get your children interested in new topics? What haven't you talked about with your children that you believe you should discuss with them?

d. When are *you* the happiest at home with your children?

Using the parents' responses to these questions as a base, talk further about the importance of parent approval of and involvement in their children's lives, using the comments in this chapter as a support for the points you stress.

With Chapter Seven—Future Goals, Future Quests

QUESTION A: WHAT WOULD YOU LIKE TO LEARN ABOUT THAT, UP UNTIL NOW, YOU HAVEN'T HAD TIME TO EXPLORE?

1. It is the rare teacher who can provide *every* student appropriate information about *every* topic or interest area. Yet teachers need not feel inadequate if they are unable to meet each child's needs; rather, teachers should become facilitators for their students' learning by finding resource persons who can provide information on beavers, or Mars' lumps, or book binding, or local history.

   Often, the public or school library will maintain a "Community Resource File"—an annotated bibliography of local persons who specialize in various crafts, topics, or out-of-school disciplines. If such a file exists, *use* it, and contact those persons who have already declared an interest in sharing their knowledge. If no file is available, or if the present file is more than three years old, develop a "resource bank" of your own with the help of your students and of the teachers. As a class assignment, ask each of your students to locate one community member who is willing to share his/her time or specialty with an individual student or a group of interested students. Find out specifics: WHAT can be shared? WHEN is the resource person available? HOW MANY pupils will s/he work with at once, and WHAT AGE child is s/he most comfortable working with?

   Most important, *utilize* these volunteers when any of your students wishes to learn about a topic that is foreign to you but, to another, is as familiar as a pair of old shoes.

2. Create a "Question of the Week" bulletin board that will expose your students to new areas of knowledge. Ask, for example:

a. "Why doesn't snow melt white if butter melts yellow and chocolate ice cream melts brown?"

b. "Why are my fingers always wrinkled when I come out of the bath-tub?"

c. "Which is smaller: a cell or an atom?"

d. "How is plastic made?"

Spark your pupils' interests by posing such questions, then, invite your students to explore for possible or definite solutions. Utilize the school library, your now-established resource file, and persons at home or in industry who might serve as ready references. Vary each week's question, thereby encouraging interests in a variety of areas. Also, invite your students to pose and post their own "Questions of the Week," giving your students a chance to share their curiosity and interest with other children.

As a small part of a classroom routine, the "Question of the Week" can serve to both find new interests and encourage those areas that students have heretofore not explored.

QUESTION B: WHAT ARE YOUR FUTURE PLANS?

1. In this section, the children who mention future careers for themselves usually select from among the obvious—doctor, lawyer, teacher, engineer, full-time parent. The child who chooses an uncommon career ("Egyptology") or combines disciplines to forge a dual career ("dancer" + "teacher" = "dance teacher") is rare.

In order to expand your students' awareness of potential careers, you can expose them to many specific, new vocations by using a readily available resource: the Yellow Pages. Begin by reviewing the pages' contents, and discover listings which seem funny (like "Rubber Consultants") or mysterious (like "Exodontists") or just plain interesting (like "Beach Pollution Controllers"). After each student has reviewed several of these "new" occupations, discover what you can about these jobs by having pupils call some persons listed under "Exodontists" (or whatever else piques their interests) to discover the specifics of the profession in question. Following these phone calls, ask each student to report back to the class the details of the occupation each has explored. Then, poll your students as to which jobs sound the most intriguing and have them call back those professionals to try to gain an in-class interview or lecture by this person.

This activity is *not* designed to dissuade students from selecting a career as a surgeon or computer programmer; rather, it is meant to expose children to areas of work which, until now, were either mysterious or unknown.

2. Thirty years ago, a career as a computer programmer did not exist. Nor, for that matter, did occupations as astronauts or laser photographers or solar energy technicians. In fact, many professions which are today commonplace were, until recently, just figments in the minds of science fiction authors.

With this information as a base, ask your students to project future occupations—those jobs that will be common in twenty years but that *today* do not exist. Also, ask them to list today's occupations that may become obsolete in the not-too-distant future, and ask for reasons for these projections. Then, have your students name those jobs which will probably *never* be automated or obsolete—gourmet chefs, perhaps, or psychologists or nurses—and ask for reasons why these jobs will always be available.

Next, investigate resources that predict future work options. *The Third Wave* (Alvin Toffler, Morrow, New York, 1980) or *Future Facts* (Stephen Rosen, Simon and Schuster, New York, 1976) or the *Occupational Outlook Handbook* (U.S. Government Department of Labor, U.S. Government Printing Office, Washington, DC, 1981) all provide clues as to what can be expected to occur in 1990 and beyond—in your *students'* futures.

There are, of course, no definites in prediction, for it is an art more than a science. However, today's discussion of tomorrow can lead to a better understanding of the logic and patterns behind our human and technological advances.

ACTIVITIES FOR FURTHER DISCUSSION

Although everyone would agree that there are "gifted mechanics" and "talented carpenters," the careers most often suggested for bright young persons are professional occupations—"white collar" jobs. Usually, long periods of advanced training or schooling precede entrance into the workaday worlds of doctors, lawyers, or college professors, yet generally there is little discussion of these "investments" prior to senior high school, if then.

The following activities are intended for use by those readers who believe that career guidance is more than a secondary school responsibility. For them, I have suggested several ways that adults can enhance the career education of gifted elementary and junior high students.

Although I do not advocate the pre-selection of a life occupation for fourth or eighth graders, I do believe that discussion of careers and methods for selecting among job options is a valid and necessary component of educating gifted children. That is the purpose behind the following group activities.

1. "Work study" is a procedure used in high schools across the country to introduce students to the world of work. Usually, a pupil will spend a portion of each school day in his or her classes ("study") and the remainder of time in active employment ("work"). This educational innovation has worked especially well for students who enter the work force immediately upon high school graduation, but it has seldom been done for bright, college-bound students. Further, work study has never applied to children younger than about sixteen years.

   However, in our efforts to expose gifted students to the array and complexity of the jobs they may be considering as a career or college major, it is important to introduce them to professions (and professionals) at an early age. For example, if a bright seventh-grader is interested in architecture, let him contact a local builder to check on the availability of visits to a construction site; if an eleven-year-old loves veterinary medicine, request that she visit an animal clinic or hospital to meet with the doctor in charge and his assistants.

   There will be those who argue that construction sites are "unsafe for kids" and that animal hospitals "will expose students to death and pain." Surely these are valid considerations; nonetheless, for the pupil (and parent or other adult) who understands and accepts these factors, a "working visit" to the location of a potential career choice could add immeasurably to a child's understanding of the reality involved with practicing a profession.

2. At times, adults or past experiences place barriers between a child's goal and its attainment. Parents and teachers sometimes direct bright children towards careers which are safe or where success is guaranteed; at other times, gifted children select a career path out of an ignorance that alternatives *do* exist.

   Ask your students the following questions, and through subsequent discussion, determine what barriers may be placed in the way of persons who choose to differ from the mainstream as regards career choice.

   a. Are there occupations that are "male" or "female"? Are there some careers that either men or women should *not* enter merely because of their sex?

   b. Are there specific careers towards which gifted children should be directed? What careers (if any) should gifted children *not* consider?

   c. At what point should a young person decide "what s/he wants to be when s/he grows up"?

   d. How will you know if you are making "success" in your life?

With Chapter Eight—
Letters: Learning From Others

GIFTED CHILDREN WRITING TO OTHER GIFTED CHILDREN

1. Most of the children in this section write letters commenting on the benefits of gifted programs. Some provide clues for coping with teachers and friends who don't seem to appreciate academic talents, while others warn incoming program members that a gifted program means more work—but work that *challenges* rather than merely fills time.

   Ask your students to write their own letter to a friend who will soon be entering their gifted program. In each letter, comments concerning the high points and drawbacks of inclusion in a program for smart students should be reviewed. When the letters are completed, read them aloud and discuss their contents in terms of your students' impressions of their own gifted program.

2. Ask each of your students to recall:
   a. their impressions of your school's gifted program *before* they entered it
   b. their initial reactions to the gifted program after their early days and weeks of involvement in it
   c. their present opinion of their gifted program in relation to previous thoughts of its merits, flaws, etc.

   Review, then, whether any of your students can predict a time when they will no longer need or desire a gifted program. What conditions—in them or in the classroom—might bring on this future reaction?

GIFTED CHILDREN WRITING TO ME

1. Ask each of your students to select his or her favorite letter in this section—the letter that answered some questions, or raised some issues, that got each pupil to thinking the most deeply about his or her abilities or attitudes *about* being bright. After your students have selected these letters, ask that each of them respond in a letter or poem or song or picture to the author of the letter each has selected. Make this response a special "thank you" for having been a source of learning or growth.

2. As a teacher, you have both academic and personal goals for your students—but have you ever revealed to *them* what these goals are? If you have, ask them to recollect what you told them, and then ask that each student evaluate how close s/he is to attaining your goals. If you have not stated explicitly to your students what goals you have for them, do so now, and benefit from your pupils' reactions to these goals.

. . . AND ONE LETTER FROM A TEACHER

1. Write a "P.S." Each of your students, and you, should mentally compose a letter that would be sent to someone on the topic of being gifted. Do not write the letter, just its "P.S."

   After completing this assignment, shuffle the P.S.'s and read each aloud, trying to guess what the author "wrote" in the letter s/he just composed in his or her head. Finally, check your hunches for each writer who volunteers his or her identity.

   (A sample "P.S." might be: "P.S. Even though there are some hassles involved with being bright, overall it's great to be smart!")

2. In this final chapter, an eleven-year-old girl took each letter in the words "A GIFTED PERSON" and described herself in terms of positive and negative feelings about being bright. Invite your students to use this format to describe themselves, using the letters in their first and surnames as the "base" from which to write their judgments. Tell your pupils that their lists might relate to any of the topics in this book—getting along

with peers, teachers, or parents; self expectations; past happinesses or future quests. Save these lists for another time, perhaps two or three months later. Then, examine the responses again, and ask your students to react to their former views of themselves. Change those items that are outdated, and retain those impressions that still apply. If time and interest allow, repeat this project intermittently throughout the school year.

A "P.S." of My Own

P.S. Over the past year I have spent much time talking with gifted children. I have spoken with dozens in person and hundreds more in writing. Expecting to find the typical gifted child somewhere among these thousands, I instead decided that there *was* no such character; that despite the intellectual signals of giftedness—early reading, advanced vocabulary, varied and intense interests—the children who shared these characteristics were still a diverse group. Also, I discovered what was *not* so obvious to me: that gifted children's abilities to learn rapidly, to deduce logically, or to think creatively all were of minor importance unless accompanied with a clear understanding of what "being gifted" means.

So, thanks to the candor and honesty of my young respondents, compiling *Gifted Children Speak Out* became one of my own most memorable learning experiences. I learned from the children about their struggles as well as their triumphs. I learned from the children that making good friends was not always as easy as making good grades. I learned, too, that I had to reexamine my own stereotypes about who a "gifted child" was and what a "gifted program" should offer. Overall, the children provided me with a reality sometimes missing in college courses and texts: that the most important part of "gifted child education" is the child.

—JIM DELISLE

For Further Reading

Does This Mean My Kid's a Genius? by Linda Perigo Moore. McGraw-Hill, Inc., New York, 1981. 193 pages.

This is *not* a recipe book which will tell you how to raise a child's IQ by implementing different parenting strategies. Instead, it is a guide for parents whose child is already quicker and more energetic and inquisitive than most. There is concrete information on definitions of giftedness, identification strategies and in-school program alternatives for bright youngsters. The writing style is light and easy-going, as Ms. Moore adds a personal perspective to enhance many of her major points.

G/C/T Magazine. G/C/T Publications, Box 66707, Mobile, Alabama 36606.

G/C/T Magazine (Gifted/Creative/Talented) is published five times per year. Each issue contains about a dozen feature articles on some aspect of teaching or living with bright children. Regular columns include "G/C/T Reviews," in which educational materials and games are critiqued; "Marji Cards," a set of three activities for use with gifted children; and "Double Perspective," a point/counterpoint column reviewing a current issue in parenting or teaching the gifted. A special feature, "Summer Activities for the Gifted," is an annual showcase (in the May/June issue) of day and residential programs for gifted children and teens.

Gifted Children Newsletter. Gifted and Talented Publications, P.O. Box 115, Sewell, New Jersey 08080.

This monthly publication is filled with practical ideas for parents of gifted children. One or two special reports are included in each issue, with such diverse topics as "Counseling Your Gifted Child," "Dealing with Sibling Rivalry," and "Books for Gifted Readers." In addition, there are excerpts from articles published elsewhere that are of interest to parents of gifted children. "Ask the Experts" is a monthly column in which leading educators and psychologists answer a question posed by a parent. For the children, a three-page series of activities and word puzzles is included in each issue.

Guiding the Gifted Child by James T. Webb, Elizabeth Meck-Stroth and Stephanie Tolan. Ohio Psychology Publishing Company, Columbus, Ohio, 1982. 262 pages.

The three co-authors bring together their diverse backgrounds as psychologist, counselor and children's book author to create a handbook that is both practical and theoretically sound. Separate chapters address issues such as peer relations, depression, and adult expectations of gifted children. Each chapter also contains a series of sample questions parents might raise regarding their gifted children; the authors provide varied responses and alternative solutions to each question raised. In 1983, the American Psychological Association gave *Guiding the Gifted Child* its Best Book of the Year Award as an outstanding contribution to the field of applied psychology.

The Hurried Child by David Elkind. Addison-Wesley Publishing Co., Inc., Reading, Massachusetts, 1981. 210 pages.

Although not related specifically to the development of gifted children, *The Hurried Child* is a useful reference for parents who are concerned that their children are being forced to grow up too fast. Elkind points out many ways in which youngsters have been transformed into "little adults" by academic, societal and parental expectations, and he then provides suggestions for helping maintain childhood as a special and unique stage of human development. For parents of gifted children, *The Hurried Child* serves as a reminder that despite high ability or talent, gifted youngsters are *still* children.

BOOKS FOR TEACHERS

Giftedness, Conflict and Underachievement by Joanne Rand Whitmore. Allyn & Bacon, Inc., Boston, 1980. 462 pages.

This textbook provides proof that the phenomenon of underachievement in gifted children is neither totally debilitating nor irreversible. Using case studies and research, the author explains underlying causes of academic and social maladjustment. Next, she reviews methods for reversing underachievement through strategies that can be implemented by classroom teachers or teachers of the gifted. A thorough review of research studies in self-concept/self-esteem and gifted child education is also included.

Inviting School Success by William Purkey. Wadsworth, Inc., Belmont, California, 1978. 98 pages.

Everything a teacher does—every smile and frown, laugh and yell, instruction given and grade recorded—is either an invitation or a disinvitation to learn. Students are keen to these cues, and in his short book, Purkey points out ways that teachers can attend to the subtle messages they send to pupils through their comments, actions and reactions.

One Hundred Ways to Enhance Self-Concept in the Classroom by Jack Canfield and Harold C. Wells. Prentice-Hall, Inc., Englewood Cliffs, New Jersey, 1976. 180 pages.

This book provides exactly what it states: one hundred strategies for developing positive self-images in children and teenagers. The activities suggested are simple, self-contained lessons all sharing the common theme of respect: respect for children's individual strengths, differences and unique qualities. Each lesson is classroom-tested and the explanation of each lesson is clearly written. A useful and extensive bibliography of books, curriculum materials and periodicals emphasizing self-concept development and a listing of organizations are also included.

The Roeper Review. Roeper City and Country School, Bloomfield Hills, Michigan 48013.

A quarterly journal devoted to gifted child education, *Roeper Review* is the most comprehensive periodical available for persons interested in current trends and research involving gifted children. Each issue has two theme sections (for example, "Pre-School Giftedness" or "The Learning Disabled Gifted Child") containing articles written by leading educational researchers or practitioners. Also, there are numerous reviews of curriculum materials, gifted program descriptions, a summary of recent doctoral research in gifted child education and a special section for parents of gifted children. *Roeper Review* is expertly edited and is always useful, informative and interesting to read.

Teaching Models in Education of the Gifted by C. June Maker. Aspen Systems Corp., Rockville, Maryland, 1982. 492 pages.

In recent years, numerous program models and curriculum designs have been devised for gifted learners. *Teaching Models* is the one text where each of these formats is explained clearly, leaving the reader with a thorough understanding of the strengths and drawbacks of each model. Among the models described are Guilford's "Structure of the Intellect," Renzulli's "Enrichment Triad" and Taylor's "Multiple Talent Approach." Although the price of this book is high, the material contained in it is valuable to teachers responsible for teaching gifted children.

Zen and the Art of Motorcycle Maintenance by Robert M. Pirsig. William Morrow & Co., Inc., New York, 1974. 412 pages.

Sometimes, in our search for *the* curriculum, *the* set of instructional materials or *the* classroom strategy that will excite each of our students, we find ourselves wanting for personal or professional fulfillment. Although there are many ways to maintain or regain our enthusiasm for teaching, I know of no better way than that of using the formula put forth in this book. Pirsig tells the tale of a man in search of quality—in his work and in his relationships with others. We become part of the personal pilgrimage of a man striving to define such elusive concepts as "truth" and "justice," and along the way we meet many characters who prevent him from reaching his goal. The parallels with the career of any dedicated professional are numerous. Busy teachers could do themselves a favor by taking the time to read *Zen and the Art of Motorcycle Maintenance.*